THE CASE INTERVIEW: 20 DAYS TO ACE THE CASE

To candidates,
We hope this book gives you confidence as you undertake the
challenging path ahead. Remember, there is a light at the end of the
tunnel: a rewarding career in consulting. Best of luck!

THE CASE INTERVIEW

20 DAYS
TO ACE THE CASE

*Your Day-by-Day Prep Course to Land
a Job in Management Consulting*

DESTIN WHITEHURST
& ERIN ROBINSON

TYCHO
PRESS

Contents

Introduction

You walk into a conference room. At a table sit a man and a woman wearing jet-black custom suits and shiny designer shoes. Their body language is casual, their gaze amicable but piercing. Behind them is the city skyline framed by the 55th floor window, a view full of optimism and promise. All that stands between you and your professional future is a 45-minute case interview, during which you must convince the two interviewers that you've got what it takes. But the real question is, have you convinced yourself?

Over the next 20 days, we will teach you how to think, speak, and act like a consultant. We will share the techniques and frameworks you need to know to nail the case interview. We will show you that the case interview is not only about the answers you give, but also about the questions you ask.

Before you begin three weeks of intense case interview preparation, you need to know that the interview is only the first of many challenges that lie ahead in your career as a management consultant. Clients demand perfection from their consultants and pay a premium to get it. A consultant's lifestyle is simultaneously glamorous and exhausting, the epitome of a work-hard, play-hard mentality. Consider the pros and cons of the industry you hope to enter:

Pros:

Thinking like a CEO: Regardless of whether you plan to enter consulting for 2 years or 20, the experience will teach you a way of problem solving that applies to any industry, service, or career. Rest assured, the world is yours for the taking once you make it into a top-tier consulting firm.

Not your typical corporate ladder: Your promotion doesn't rely on someone else advancing or retiring. Consulting firms want to make as many partners as possible because people are their assets. More people means they can generate more revenue.

Constant change: Most strategy consulting projects last 2 to 6 months. What, where, and with whom you work change constantly. The fast pace forces you to learn quickly, and it will prevent you from getting bored, frustrated, or stuck in a professional rut.

Coffee shops, pajamas, and beaches: What do these three things have in common? They represent a consultant's flexible workplace. Unlike a "normal" job, as a consultant you will rarely find yourself in the confines of a cubicle. When you're not working in a client's boardroom with team-mates, you can work in a coffee shop or even in bed.

The corporate expense card: Most consultants travel 48 weeks out of the year, all expenses covered. On weekends, many consulting firms allow you to travel anywhere you want, within reason, on their dime (they would've paid for you to go home anyway). Also, you will accrue substantial airline, hotel, and credit card reward points to use at your disposal.

Cons:

Nights, weekends, and the smartphone that never sleeps: Consulting is not a 9-to-5 job. Expect to work an average of 50 to 60 hours per week, sometimes more. Granted, it's not investment banking or a medical residency, but you will work hard.

"The Sunday Blues": A mild anxiety may creep up on you each Sunday in anticipation of that 6:00 a.m. Monday morning flight. Unfortunately, you will become familiar with that anxiety as a new consultant. Don't worry, though: The feeling goes away by Monday afternoon.

You may not be getting a dog anytime soon: The travel is constant and unforgiving. Friends learn quickly not to call you for happy hour. Significant others get familiar with Skype and FaceTime. If you're single or live alone, having a pet (or a plant, for that matter) can be a challenge. Sometimes traveling is sexy; sometimes you just want to go home.

Now is the time to ask yourself: Why do I want to be a consultant? Do the pros outweigh the cons? What do I hope to accomplish in the next five years? Am I willing to prepare myself for a daunting interview process that leaves little room for error?

Hopefully, the answer to this last question is a resounding "yes."

As a supplement to your interview preparation process, this book is designed to provide structure and rigor in the final days leading up to your case interview. To reach your full potential, you should have already dedicated many hours to preparing for your case interview. Over the next 20 days, you should read one chapter each day leading up to your interview, fully absorbing the content and lessons from each. Over the course of the program, you will complete nine mock case interviews, learn about frameworks, and gain dozens of game-changing tips and tricks to help you be successful, both on interview day and throughout your career as a consultant.

As case interview preparation can be taxing, keep yourself in the best health possible throughout the process so you can get to your interview in top mental and physical state. Over the next few weeks, we encourage you to eat nutritious, well-balanced meals with brain-boosting foods, exercise regularly, and get plenty of rest every night.

It's also important to practice as many cases as possible in front of an audience. Ask a parent or friend to act as your mock interviewer, using this book as a guide. This will allow you to answer the questions as you would on interview day. The true test of your success won't be reading the case and understanding the answers given; it will be learning to organize your thoughts and give eloquent responses under pressure. To facilitate your live practice with a partner and encourage you to think on your own and go off-script, we've provided interview guides (see Appendix A, page 166) for each of the nine cases.

The fact that you are reading this book means the odds are already stacked in your favor. Let's assume that one hundred candidates applied for the consulting position, thirty were invited to interview, and only five people will be extended offers. This is the typical funneling process of consulting recruiting, and you will be competing with the best and the brightest members of your academic class. With this book, you'll increase your chances of acing the interview. You'll learn lessons and insights that come directly from management consultants and case interview experts—advice that has led to interview success for many consultants before you. Discipline, repetition, and exposure to different cases, as well as building and polishing your live case interview skills, will be required to be successful at the interview. Are you ready for this?

Take a deep breath and let's begin.

20 19 18 17 16 15

14 13 12 11 10 9 8

7 6 5 4 3 2 1

20

How to Listen with Intent

What makes a case interview equal parts beauty and beast? It's the multitude of intangible factors that your interviewer assesses throughout the interview. As you analyze data and deliver your assessments, a storm of inquiries rages inside your interviewer's mind: Does this person have poise? Can this person think on her feet? How does this person handle pressure? What nonverbal cues does this person give off? Is this person a good listener?

The last question is especially important. Listening skills will undoubtedly make or break your interview.

Let me be clear: listening is not synonymous with hearing. Listening means taking in a variety of information and comprehending all of it. During the interview, you will be given a lot of information, and quickly. The key is to understand the data you have and recognize the data you are missing.

Certainly, consulting firms recruit at Ivy League schools. However, the top firms hire from countless other universities across the country and world. Firms look for talent wherever it may be found.

One common pitfall is rambling simply to fill the silence. Socially, we may have been taught to never allow stale air into a conversation. Rambling, however, is no solution and you must conquer this habit before your case interview. To become a good listener and, more importantly, to have a successful case interview, you must become comfortable with silence. As you engage and interact with your interviewer, embrace periods of "quiet time." You will need this time to organize the information at hand and make sure you truly understand the question asked.

The Case Prompt

Listen first for dates, dollar figures, and certain keywords, such as "declining growth," "increasing competition," "new regulations," or other terms that shed light on the business challenges. Jot down notes in shorthand so you can refer to them easily later in the interview.

At the end of the prompt, the interviewer will pose an initial question to you. Listen carefully for the exact question being asked. Jot the question down in its entirety.

After the interviewer finishes speaking, recite back the key facts you heard. This will ensure that you correctly noted the dates, dollar figures, and keywords used to describe the case. Most importantly, recite back the question to make certain you understood correctly. You don't want to get to the middle of the interview and find out that you've been solving for declining revenue when, in fact, the case prompt asked you to solve for declining profit.

Once you're certain you noted all of the information correctly, ask for a moment to collect your thoughts. What do you know? What do you *not* know? If you were consulting for the client firm, what follow-up questions would you have for them? Ask the interviewer your own questions for clarification or probing.

The Framework

You'll also need to think like an investigator and determine the information your interviewer might be withholding. The key to recognizing missing facts is thinking formulaically. Listen for gaps in the story and prepare follow-up questions.

Let's say you're asked to determine the market size for American-manufactured luxury automobiles in Brazil. After asking your initial questions, it becomes apparent that this is an extremely attractive opportunity. Why would the client need a consultant for something so obvious? What information might she be withholding? It could be a multitude of things, such as high import tariffs, unattainable emissions standards, or corrupt customs regimes. You may have to look at several

MY INTERVIEW STORY

"I was nervous when I received an invitation to interview at Accenture. I didn't know what to expect, even after the recruiters provided me with an overview of the interview process. I went through four rounds of interviews, and each time I was greeted by friendly consultants who made me feel more comfortable. The toughest part of the process was the skills portion of the interview because I had no prior consulting experience. Luckily, I received a good piece of advice going into the interview: to be myself because consulting is less about the hard skills you possess and more about how well you can adapt and work with others. Today, I am three years into my career as a consultant and I couldn't agree with that advice more!"

Jen S., Technology Consultant, Accenture

SET YOURSELF UP

Performing well on the case interview is a requirement for getting a job in consulting. At a minimum, you must prove that you have the intellect to work among the best and brightest men and women in business. However, acing the case interview may not be enough to land an offer. Beyond the case interview, there are actions you can take to set yourself up for success.

Network like a Professional

Arguably the most important action, networking helps you accomplish three goals: (1) it shows your interest in the firm, (2) it rallies support before the interview, and (3) it helps you learn more about the firm you're pursuing. Networking also shows that you're proactive and confident. Start by reaching out to junior practitioners (typically called analysts or associates). Junior practitioners remember what it's like to be in your shoes—they were there only a few years ago. Learn from their advice. Next, ask to be introduced to a more senior practitioner (typically called managers or partners). Always accommodate the professionals' schedule, and come prepared with specific questions and conversation topics. Networking might be intimidating, but ultimately it will take some of the pressure off your actual interview and increase your chances of being considered for the job.

Do Your Research

It's important to know what a consultant does and what the firm is like. When was it founded? Who is the CEO? What markets does it serve? Who are its

different angles, asking your interviewer a variety of questions before discovering the true nature of the case given.

If your interviewer doesn't have any additional information to share, ask yourself: What can I safely assume? What can I infer? As you work through the case, don't hesitate to allow yourself more "quiet time" to collect your thoughts and review the information. As you discuss the case, make sure that you're bringing the interviewer along on the journey main competitors? Has it gone through any major restructuring or consolidation in the last several years? The Internet is a good resource for answers to these questions. Also, check out *The Lords of Strategy* by Walter Kiechel III, which gives a history of consulting and its key players. For fun, watch a few episodes of the Showtime series *House of Lies*. The show is a mix of fact and fiction, but it will give you an idea of the profession.

Polish Your Story

Before going into the interview, draft a two-minute "elevator pitch" about who you are and why you want to be a consultant. Practice walking through your résumé with someone in a clear, succinct way. Make sure you are able to answer the following questions: Why do I want to be a consultant? Why do I want to work for your target firm? What makes me uniquely qualified to work there? What do I envision for my career in five years? Ten years? Thirty years? The behavioral portion of the interview is equally as important as the case interview. You need to be comfortable promoting yourself in a way that's true to who you are. Be humble, but don't shy away from speaking to your accomplishments. Also, be prepared to talk about the motivations behind any key experiences: Why did I choose to join the student senate? What motivated me to start my own nonprofit? What spawned my love for sports?

by stating the assumptions and inferences you've made and that you're following your initial framework.

As you will learn in more detail later in the book, case interviews test your ability to balance asking questions and making inferences. Sometimes your interviewer will have additional information, sometimes she won't. However, she certainly won't give it to you unless you ask for it.

Interview Wrap-Up

Listen for cues on how the interviewer would like you to conclude. Does she want you to summarize at a high level? Does she want you to dive deeper into a particular topic? Does she ask for your final recommendation, or does she want a list of options?

This part serves as your last chance to show your interviewer that you've grasped the concepts of the case and are able to organize your thoughts to form a recommendation. Within those confines, the interviewer may direct you as to how she wants you to finish. Listen carefully so that you end on a high note.

Honing Your Listening Skills

When you're a good listener, you will appear more poised, adaptable, and calm under pressure. You will project thoughtful cues and show your interviewer that you know how to logically organize your thoughts.

Listening is important during the case interview because it's an essential trait of a good consultant. Sometimes when you work with clients, you may feel more like a therapist than a business partner. Throughout most of the project, clients talk and consultants listen.

FIRM PROFILE: DELOITTE CONSULTING

The only Big Four firm to consistently retain a full consulting practice, Deloitte leverages its suite of professional services—audit, consulting, enterprise risk, financial advisory, and tax—to solve clients' most complex challenges. The consulting arm is organized into three areas: human capital, strategy and operations, and technology. Through their combined expertise, Deloitte works with its clients from initial strategy design to project implementation.

Listening to clients allows you to build strong relationships with them and to identify areas of the business that require attention. Their daily challenges shed light on new ideas. Similarly, listening carefully during the case interview will build rapport between you and your interviewer and allow you to give more organized, deliberate answers.

LEARNING TARGETS:

◎ *Jot down dates, dollar figures, and keywords that highlight any business challenges during the case prompt.*

◎ *Think like an investigator. Consider what information the interviewer might be withholding and prepare follow-up questions.*

◎ *Listen for cues as to how you should conclude the case.*

19

Breaking the Case Down

You will deal with a lot of information during the case interview. At times, it will feel like you're drinking from a fire hydrant. The key to not becoming overwhelmed is this: learn how to break the case down into bite-size chunks of information that are easily digestible.

Later in this book, you will learn frameworks and techniques that apply to particular types of cases or questions. The basic concepts covered in this chapter are fundamental ways of thinking that you should apply to each and every case, regardless of type. Master these concepts before applying more specific frameworks later on.

With that, let's introduce you to your new **BFF**:

- **B**aby steps
- **F**ull cognition
- **F**unneled thinking

These three concepts will allow you to process complex information more easily and transform a daunting problem into a solvable riddle. Tomorrow, as you execute your first mock case interview, remember to incorporate the concepts from this chapter.

Baby Steps

Your primary challenge in a case interview isn't to find an answer to a particular question; it's to show your interviewer how you got to your answer. Think of it this way: the case is a journey, not a destination. The best way to navigate that journey is to take small steps, thoughtfully explaining your logic and reasoning to your interviewer in simple and clear increments. Doing so forces you to slow down your thinking. In turn, it prevents you from getting ahead of yourself and losing your interviewer along the way.

You can think of the process as akin to learning algebra in school. Teachers graded based on the work shown. Even if the final answer was incorrect, they gave points for executing the mathematical procedures correctly. The same logic applies to the case interview. Taking baby steps is like showing your work to your interviewer. Even if your final answer isn't the solution the case needs, the interviewer can follow your logic and understand the reasoning behind your alternative solution. You are opening a window into your mind's inner workings, which is the fundamental purpose of the case interview.

FIRM PROFILE: A.T. KEARNEY

Formerly a branch of McKinsey & Company, A.T. Kearney has grown from its original focus of operations and manufacturing to include standard consulting services like technology, mergers and acquisitions, innovation, and strategy. Renowned for studying trends across a wide range of industries, the firm releases annual reports such as the Global Retail Development Index, which details retail trends in markets worldwide.

"MBB" stands for McKinsey, Bain, and BCG. Also known as the Big Three, these companies are often considered to be the most prestigious firms in the industry due to their role in consulting's inception, their treatment in business media, and the C-suite access commanded by each.

Full Cognition

The brain has two systems for thinking about and judging situations: intuition and reasoning. The case interview requires you to engage both systems. We call this full cognition.

Intuition kicks in quickly and effortlessly. Your instincts and emotions work together to make automatic judgments and associations based on your past experiences. Reasoning is slower and more controlled. With some effort, your brain takes in all the information at hand to draw rational, data-driven conclusions. Reasoning neutralizes your emotions and serves as a gatekeeper for what you feel, say, or do.

During the case interview, both intuition and reasoning will help you come up with creative and justified recommendations. To use them in harmony, try the following:

1. Recognize your intuition.
2. Follow your reasoning.
3. Test your reasoning against your intuition.

At the beginning of the case, your intuition will kick in. Try to recognize the initial "gut reactions" you have to the case prompt. What feels off about the situation? What questions immediately pop into your mind? What does the situation remind you of, if anything? While acknowledging these thoughts, don't speak or jump into questioning. This is where reasoning takes over.

Ask your interviewer for a moment to collect your thoughts. Review the notes you took during the case prompt, and begin to process the information. After reciting the facts back to your interviewer and asking several rational questions, take a silent moment to follow your reasoning. To organize your thoughts, come up with a framework. A framework is an established method for exploring the case. (You will learn more about frameworks later in the book.)

As the case progresses, periodically test your reasoning against your intuition. Does it feel like something is missing? Have you gone down one logical path but abandoned a more obvious solution? You may find that your gut is telling you one thing, but your rational mind is silencing it.

Intuition and reasoning can be refined and improved. With more experience comes better intuition. With more knowledge comes better reasoning. As Louis Pasteur said, "Chance favors the prepared mind."

MY INTERVIEW STORY

"I arrived at my fourth of six BCG interviews feeling confident. I was interviewing with a principal, and the topic was how to increase profits in the restaurant business. I thought the case would be easy, but it turned out to be my toughest interview. I framed the question correctly and approached it with a reasonable framework, but for some reason I could not come up with the 'right' solution. Each solution, from simple to elaborate, was rejected by the interviewer. I left the interview feeling exhausted, and my confidence had dwindled. Fortunately, I was invited to the final two rounds. Later, the interviewer told me that the previous interview was a 'stress test' and to succeed, the candidate must persevere regardless of how many times the solution is rejected and to show a sense of calm and poise under stress."

Dyota M., Associate, Boston Consulting Group

Funneled Thinking

As with most situations in business, there's rarely one answer to a given problem in the case interview. Zooming in on one solution for a problem and ignoring possible alternatives is a common mistake that many unprepared candidates make. Therefore, always approach the case with an open mind, capturing as many angles as possible before focusing on a specific approach. Rather than producing a single answer, start with widespread, high-level responses, and gradually narrow in on more specific, detailed solutions as you receive more data. This is called "funneled thinking." It will be especially important at the beginning and end of the case, during the introductory and wrap-up sections.

The interviewer is primarily looking for a candidate's breadth of knowledge and ability to think at a high level. Once that's established, the interviewer tests the candidate's ability to dive deep into a particular subject. Typically, the case prompt at the beginning of an interview will pose a broad and sweeping qualitative challenge. Start by brainstorming possible roots of the challenge. Your focus should be on coming up with a list of solutions that are Mutually Exclusive and Collectively Exhaustive (MECE).

After you've explored all the MECE options with your interviewer, pause for a moment. Your interviewer may steer you in a different direction or may ask you to elaborate on one of your responses. Either way, you will home in on more specific answers as the interview progresses.

TIP: LIVE PRACTICE

For live practice, begin scheduling mock interviews with a parent, friend, or a consulting interview coach today. You will have a mock interview every other day for the next two and a half weeks, so pick the best days for you and your interviewer to practice.

During your final recommendation, summarize the topics covered before explaining how your framework helped you identify the best solution. Review your funneled thinking for your interviewer so that she sees the breadth and depth of your ability to solve problems.

CASE INTERVIEW IN

18

DAYS

Mock Interview No. 1

Read through the following script with a friend or classmate. Next, review the instructions for live case practice on page 166. When ready, have your partner use the interview guide on page 167 to lead you through the case as if it were an actual interview.

Interviewer: *Our client, BullDoze Inc., is a heavy machinery manufacturer based in Indiana. Over the past five years, BullDoze has seen average annual revenue growth of 12 percent while operating in 24 markets in South America, Africa, and the Middle East. However, revenue growth across those geographies is projected to drop by 50 percent within the next three years. In response, our client has begun to search for new growth opportunities in emerging markets. One such opportunity may exist in southeast Asia, and BullDoze Inc. has asked us to analyze the market to determine if the company should expand into the area.*

Candidate: Do you mind if I take a few seconds to organize my notes?

Interviewer: *Sure, take your time.*

Candidate: Okay, I understand that our client is BullDoze Inc., a heavy machinery manufacturer based in the United States that has enjoyed 12 percent annual revenue growth over the last five years. However, due to projections of slowing demand in its current geographies over the next three years, the client is potentially interested in entering new markets with more sales potential. One market that has already been identified by the client is southeast Asia. Is that correct?

Interviewer: *We actually don't know if the reduction in revenue growth is due to lower demand or other reasons like competitive pricing. The rest of your statement was accurate.*

Candidate: Ah, thank you for that clarification. I'd like to learn a bit more about BullDoze Inc. What exactly does the company sell, and who are its typical customers?

Interviewer: *Our client sells heavy machinery used for construction sites, such as backhoes and bulldozers. Nearly 80 percent of its customers are construction companies, about 15 percent are governments, and 5 percent are individuals, such as farmers or ranchers.*

Candidate: Do we know why the client is interested in southeast Asia specifically?

Interviewer: *According to several media outlets, the governments of Cambodia, Myanmar, Thailand, and Vietnam are on the verge of announcing plans to build an international highway system to better facilitate trade. The system will stretch to all four corners of the region, leading to India in the northwest and China in the northeast. Initial construction is expected to begin within the next two years.*

Candidate: Interesting. Can I take a minute to collect my thoughts and jot down some notes?

Interviewer: *Of course.*

Candidate: In considering if BullDoze Inc. should enter the southeast Asian market, there are three things I'd like to analyze. I'll start with general concerns and then focus from there. First, I'd like to determine if the opportunity is large enough to have a substantial effect on BullDoze's revenue growth. Second, I'd like to learn more about the competitive landscape in the area, specifically how competition might affect which company wins the contract for providing equipment to the highway project. Third, I'd want to learn whether it would be cost-effective for our client's supply chain to support a major project in an area so far from BullDoze's traditional sphere of business.

Interviewer: *That sounds like a good list to me.*

Candidate: Perfect. Starting with opportunity size, do we know BullDoze Inc.'s average revenue per year? What is the projected size of the new project in terms of revenue potential?

Interviewer: *The client's revenue last year was $5 billion. We don't have exact numbers on the potential construction equipment spend for the project, but we do know that the overall budget for the new highway system is nearly $10 billion.*

Candidate: Okay. Let's assume that of that $10 billion, 80 percent will be spent on land rights, materials, construction crews, management, and other costs. That leaves 20 percent, or $2 billion, for actual construction equipment. Does that sound reasonable?

Interviewer: *It does.*

Candidate: Great. That $2 billion represents 40 percent of our client's current revenue, so it definitely warrants BullDoze's interest.

Interviewer: *What about the timeline? How might that affect the attractiveness of the project?*

Candidate: Ah. Well, if the project lasted five years, then the $2 billion in total revenue would be divided into $400 million a year, which isn't incredibly attractive when you consider the company's average annual revenue. However, based on what I know about highway construction, I'm going to assume that it takes a maximum of two years to complete the bulk of the initial work, such as land clearing and excavation. As BullDoze's products are designed to complete this type of work, is it fair to assume that the initial two-year phase is most relevant for BullDoze?

Interviewer: *It is.*

Candidate: Great. So even at $1 billion in revenue per year, the deal would represent a clear growth opportunity for BullDoze. Let's move on to the competitive landscape. Is there any risk that the governments involved already have a company contracted to provide the equipment? Who are the major players in the area?

Interviewer: *The governments have formed a coalition and have held some discussions with the construction equipment industry leaders. Both of the main competitors are global players that focus predominately on the developed markets in North America, Europe, Australia, and Japan. While it seems that no company has yet been awarded the contract, we have no insight into whether or not negotiations have already begun.*

Candidate: How do their prices compare to BullDoze's?

Interviewer: *These specific competitors have the most advanced, powerful equipment available and charge a premium. Their prices are 20 percent higher than our client's.*

Candidate: How does their equipment's effectiveness compare to BullDoze's?

Interviewer: *Their equipment has an average lifespan that is 20 percent longer and engines that are nearly 10 percent more powerful.*

Candidate: I'm not a construction expert, but neither of those characteristics seem to be deal breakers. In fact, it sounds like BullDoze may have two competitive advantages that could be leveraged to earn the contract.

First, BullDoze has experience in emerging markets, which could be attractive to the government coalition. Such experience means that BullDoze will have a practical view of the costs, corruption, and labor productivity typically seen in the developing world.

Second, BullDoze's prices are much more enticing, assuming that the coalition is sensitive to price. Let's dive a bit deeper. What about distribution costs? Does our client have any factories nearby where it could cheaply produce the equipment, or would it need to build a facility?

Interviewer: *The closest manufacturing plant is in Pakistan, on the Indian Ocean coast. The cost to ship one piece of construction equipment, such as a bulldozer, is $100 per mile. There are roughly 3,000 miles between the factory and the nearest port in southeast Asia.*

Candidate: All right, we need to figure out what the total shipping cost would be should BullDoze use its Pakistan facility. Right now, we know that the cost to ship one unit of equipment is equal to $100 per mile multiplied by 3,000 miles, or $300,000. Let's assume that there will be 1,000 pieces of equipment involved in the project. We multiply our $300,000 by 1,000 units and end up with $30 million.

Interviewer: *Hmm, I'm getting a different number. Can you run me through that math one more time?*

Candidate: Oh, sorry. I think I left off a zero. It should be $300 million.

Interviewer: *Exactly.*

Candidate: And what's the cost for building a new manufacturing facility?

Interviewer: *The cost is $250 million, but can you think of another negative consideration related to building new equipment?*

Candidate: I suppose the time it takes to build a facility could affect BullDoze's ability to complete the highway project on time.

Interviewer: *Correct. It takes about three years to build a factory from scratch.*

Candidate: So $300 million is the expected cost for shipping the equipment to southeast Asia. Compared to the time delays and costs related to building a new factory, $300 million seems reasonable. Even after the shipping expense, BullDoze will earn $700 million in net income per year, which still represents more than 10 percent of current revenue.

Interviewer: *That makes sense to me. If you had more time, what are some other costs related to shipping the equipment that you'd want to know?*

Candidate: Well, there could be tariffs involved in importing the equipment. Also, there are port fees and land transportation costs that would need to be considered.

Interviewer: *Any others?*

Candidate: Perhaps the cost of ramping up production at BullDoze's manufacturing facility?

Interviewer: *Go on.*

Candidate: Well, I imagine there is limited bandwidth at the company's factory, so this new project would require longer shifts, more shifts, more physical capacity, or cannibalization of other products being produced. Longer and increased shifts would result in increased labor costs. More physical capacity would involve a capital expenditure, and the cannibalization of other products would lead to reduced sales.

Interviewer: *I agree. We don't have any information available at this time to analyze it further, but if we signed a project engagement with BullDoze, we would certainly research those costs further. Bringing it back to a general view, can you provide a quick summary of where we've landed?*

Candidate: Is it all right if I take a minute to organize my thoughts?

Interviewer: *Of course.*

Candidate: Great. There are three key areas we discussed while analyzing BullDoze's opportunity to expand into southeast Asia.

First, we determined that the highway-system proposal would represent 40 percent of our client's annual revenues, or $2 billion. This is an attractive option compared to the projected slow-downs in other geographic areas.

Next, we learned that the contract hasn't been awarded, and compared to the two main competitors, BullDoze has more attractive pricing, similar equipment, and more experience in emerging markets. These factors will give our client a legitimate shot at winning the contract.

Last, we estimated the main supply chain expense required to provide sufficient equipment for the project. At a cost of $300 million, the upside for BullDoze remains strong.

Interviewer: *So what is your recommendation?*

Candidate: Based on the data available, I recommend that BullDoze pursue the southeast Asia highway-system contract to boost their revenue growth potential in the near term. Leveraging its current manufacturing sites and experience in developing markets, the company is well positioned to efficiently and successfully complete the project.

Interviewer: *But what if they don't win the contract? It seems silly to base an entire growth strategy on one project that isn't even guaranteed.*

Candidate: That's a good point, though there should be ripple effects throughout the region that extend beyond the main highway. For example, more buildings like gas stations and restaurants will need to be developed along the roads to support travelers. Each of those projects would require heavy construction machinery. And there will be people who have to run those businesses, which means more housing will need to be built along the new highway as well. It's highly unlikely that one company could dominate all tangential opportunities that will be produced by the main project.

Interviewer: *Touché. If we had more time, what else would you want to know to better inform your recommendation?*

Candidate: Is it okay if I take a few seconds?

Interviewer: *Of course.*

Candidate: Given more time, I would want to analyze the other supply chain costs we mentioned, such as land transportation costs, tariffs, port fees, and production costs. I'd also want to learn more about the specifics of the contract and the growth projections for the region after the highway is complete. As I mentioned earlier, there could be numerous opportunities created by the construction of the new highway.

Interviewer: *Excellent, that completes our case. Do you have any questions for me?*

Candidate: That was an intriguing business problem. Was this an actual project? If so, how did it turn out for BullDoze?

Interviewer: *Great question. I actually worked on this engagement back when . . .*

17

Profitability Framework

You've completed your first mock case interview. How did it go? Were there any surprises? How did your answers compare to the candidate in the script? Did you apply the basic elements learned from your BFF?

There are many ways to approach a business problem, and you have eight more mock interviews to help you develop and polish your case interview skills. Hopefully, you observed how the candidate (1) took **baby steps** to walk the interviewer through his logic step-by-step, (2) used **full cognition** to give creative and rational responses, and (3) used **funneled thinking** to start with high-level responses and gradually home in on the details. As you encounter the following cases in this book, remember that these fundamental concepts will help you navigate even the most complex problems.

The typical case interview is a conversation between candidate and interviewer. A good candidate will engage with the interviewer and adapt to the information given. The candidate should also drive the interview with little-to-no major course correction from the interviewer.

To go from "good" to "great," you need to master several key business frameworks. A framework is a problem-solving methodology that guides the user to a logical answer through a formulaic approach.

The first framework we're going to share with you is the **profitability framework**:

$$\text{Revenue} - \text{Cost} = \text{Profit}.$$

What Is Revenue?

Revenue is money generated through the sale of goods or services. It is composed of two factors: price and volume. You can determine a company's revenue by multiplying the price of goods sold by the volume of goods sold.

When you're given a case that uses language associated with growth, sales, or price, you should start by inquiring about revenue and volume. What major products does the company sell? What is the typical sales volume for those products? Is it cyclical? Does the company sell more of some products than others? Has it seen any major changes in sales volume over the past few years? Don't confuse popularity with high sales. Many companies may be popular without any sales at all—think social media, popular blogs, or free iPhone apps.

FIRM PROFILE: MCKINSEY & COMPANY

Founded in 1926, McKinsey & Company originally focused on providing financial and accounting advice. They later shifted to using financial data to improve management decisions, thereby inventing the concept of consultants (or "management engineers"). The firm is one of the most recognized names in the industry, a spot achieved through active marketing of its perspective through a regular consulting brief, the McKinsey Quarterly, and think tanks such as McKinsey Global Institute. Operating as a global entity that fills its ranks with MBAs, JDs, MDs, and PhDs, McKinsey & Company has the size and scale to solve the most complex of business problems.

Next, ask your interviewer for information on the company's prices. How do they compare to a competitor's prices? Do their products sell at a premium? Do their products sell at a discount? Are their prices steady all year, or do they fluctuate? Has the company increased or decreased prices in recent years?

Price and volume are inversely related. As price increases, volume decreases. Declining revenue could be caused by a multitude of factors, but fundamentally, the company is operating outside of economic equilibrium. Either prices are too high, causing customers to purchase from competitors, or prices are too low, a problem that can be avoided if it's discovered that customers are willing to pay higher prices. Either way, the company is missing out on potential revenue.

What Is Cost?

Cost is the money spent to do business. Costs typically fall into one of two categories: fixed or variable. Fixed costs remain unchanged regardless of units sold.

Fixed costs may include:

* rent
* mortgage payments
* labor (salaries)
* insurance
* advertising
* utilities

Variable costs, which can increase as units sold increase, may include:

- raw material
- labor (wages)
- transportation (e.g., gasoline, vehicle depreciation, maintenance)
- utilities

You'll notice a slight overlap between some costs. Some utilities are considered fixed costs because they don't depend on the number of units sold. For example, a publishing company has to keep the water and electricity on in its office building regardless of how many books it sells. Other utilities are considered variable. A hotel's utility costs go up when more rooms are occupied by guests who take showers, watch TV, and use the air conditioning.

Another cost that can be either variable or fixed is labor. Typically, salaries will be a fixed cost and wages will be a variable cost. Salaries are paid regardless of hours worked or units sold. Wages, however, are directly related to hours worked, which will depend on units sold.

What Is Profit?

Profit is often referred to as a company's "bottom line." You may also hear terms such as "net income," "net loss," or "net earnings." A company is profitable when its revenue (sales, or "top line") exceed its costs ("expenses," "total costs," or "total expenses"). A company is operating at a loss when costs exceed revenue.

FACTOID

After the Enron scandal in 2001, three of the Big Four accounting firms—PricewaterhouseCoopers, KPMG, and Ernst & Young—divested their consulting arms, while Deloitte continued growing their consulting practice. Today, all four are involved in management consulting, though each focuses on a slightly different segment of the market.

Q&A WITH AN INTERVIEW EXPERT

TITLE: Engagement Manager, Global Strategy Consulting Firm
CONSULTING TENURE: Five years
CASE INTERVIEW EXPERIENCE: Five years, three campuses, two countries

Q: Can you describe the perfect case interview candidate?

The perfect candidate would be someone who enters the room with a smile and is poised, confident, and prepared with materials (e.g., notepad with grid paper, pencil or pen). We want our candidates to be able to articulate why they're interviewing to be a consultant with our firm.

During the case, listening is crucial. Ninety-nine percent of the time, the prompt doesn't have enough information. They need to ask probing questions but can't do so if they haven't listened.

They need to be able to step back and be aware of the key problem the client is facing. There is no right answer, but there is a right way to structure thoughts, incorporate feedback, and walk through the problem. The person must be able to set a framework and stick to it through the entire case. Quantitative skills and the ability to voice mental math quickly are crucial. They should always tie the answers back to the original question.

Last, they should conclude as if it were a final presentation to the client by summarizing the initial problem, providing the analysis results, and offering potential next steps.

Q: Does receiving a job offer hinge solely on the case interview?

Absolutely not. It may depend on the firm, but it's a combination of whether the candidate fits into the culture and the candidate's intellectual horsepower. Any top firm would say the candidate needs to have not just the ability to structure logically, but also the ability to interact with teams and clients. If

I were to weight the necessary qualities, it would be 60 percent case interview performance and 40 percent interpersonal skills. The case interview provides good information, but every interaction throughout the recruiting process is measured.

Q: How crucial is it that a candidate solve the case?

For me, it's crucial because candidates are in the shoes of consultants. As consultants, we're paid to provide answers. If the candidate can't act as a consultant in the interview, that's not a good reflection of their ability to perform on the job. We always come up with a recommendation and next steps to take.

Q: What are common mistakes candidates make during the case interview?

Not being prepared. Not bringing the right materials. I've had to hand a blank piece of paper to a candidate. That's a huge mistake. Not having a smile on their face—they should have fun during the case! It's good to show some personality. Also, not being able to articulate why he or she is interested in the firm. Showing visible nervousness is not good either, nor is treating the interview like a one-sided conversation.

The candidate should ask intelligent, genuine questions; this helps us determine if the candidate is a good fit. I'd rather a candidate ask about how they can grow within the firm, compared to how the firm will navigate low oil prices, for example.

Q: How are case interviews developed?

Most case interviews are real-life business cases solved for actual clients, developed by a panel of consultants that are at the level of the hiring position.

When a business earns a profit, it can either reinvest the profit back into the company or pay it out to stakeholders.

When would a company choose to reinvest and when would it choose to pay it out? The answer depends on whether a company is focused on rapid growth or steady value.

Newer, up-and-coming companies tend to focus on **growth**, reinvesting profits to expand the business. What does it mean to reinvest in the company? What types of things might a company reinvest in? A few examples are building a new manufacturing plant, hiring more employees, and expanding its online presence through more advertising.

Older, steady-state companies may focus on **value**, using profits to deliver returns to its investors in the form of dividends and stock buybacks. Value-focused companies tend to see conservative but consistent growth figures, making them an attractive investment for people who are more averse to risk.

Revenues, costs, and profits are recorded on a company's income statement. Typically, these statements come out each fiscal quarter and each fiscal year. Keep in mind that private companies operate on their own fiscal year, which may not correspond to the calendar year.

CONSULTING WISDOM

"I am passionate about social impact work, and the skills I developed in consulting have been very useful in the public sector. I spent several months working in Ethiopia to expand access to microloans for rural farmers. Drawing on the same analytic and communication skills I used to serve Fortune 500 clients in the United States, I analyzed agricultural data to predict farmer loan needs in different regions of the country and presented this information to the nation's largest microfinance institutions. The top-notch training I received in consulting prepared me to make a difference on issues that really matter to me."

Senior Associate Consultant, Bain & Company

When Should I Apply the Profitability Framework to a Case?

In the case interview, you will frequently encounter economic challenges such as slowing growth, declining profitability, or decreasing margins. When you hear this type of financial language, think of the profitability framework. Regardless of the clues the interviewer gives you, it's always best to consider all three components of the equation Revenue – Cost = Profit. To arrive at a determination for profitability, always examine the major components of both revenue and cost: price, volume, fixed costs, and variable costs.

Here's a final tip to impress your interviewer. Consultants typically show their work in presentation format, slides that employ visual aids such as charts, graphics, and formulas. Draw a simple diagram during your case interview (you can also refer to them as "slides" during your interview). In doing so, you will demonstrate logical thought and visual communication. For even more bonus points, write down the profit formula as you interact with your interviewer, holding up your paper or gesturing to your framework depiction. Remember, an interactive interview is much more interesting to the interviewer than one with no interpersonal dialogue.

LEARNING TARGETS:

◎ Apply the profitability framework (Revenue – Cost = Profit) when you encounter challenges such as slow growth, declining profitability, or decreasing margins.

◎ Inquire about revenue and volume when you're given a case about growth, sales, or prices.

◎ Understand that costs are normally categorized as fixed or variable, but sometimes there is an overlap (e.g., utilities).

◎ Discern whether a company is focused on rapid growth or steady value.

20 19 18 17 16 15

14 13 12 11 10 9 8

7 6 5 4 3 2 1

16

DAYS

Mock Interview No. 2

Read through the following script with a friend or classmate.
Next, review the instructions for live case practice on page
166. When ready, have your partner use the interview guide
on page 168 to lead you through the case as if it were an
actual interview.

Interviewer: *Body Surf Hotel was founded 15 years ago by four*
Canadian coworkers who wanted to swap their comfortable cor-
porate lifestyles for something more entrepreneurial and less
structured. Operating in three Central American countries, the
hotel provides cabana lodging and private surf lessons. Historically,
the majority of Body Surf Hotel's guests have been health-conscious
young adults from the United States and Canada. Leading their
region in social media marketing, the company has enjoyed increas-
ingly high levels of popularity. However, over the past few years the
company has struggled to earn a profit. They've enlisted our help to
identify the issue and provide a set of potential solutions.

Candidate: Interesting. Do you mind if I take a minute to organize my notes?

Interviewer: **No problem.**

Candidate: Okay, I'm going to repeat the data you provided to ensure that I haven't missed any details. My understanding is that our client is Body Surf Hotel, a Central American company offering private surf lessons and cabana lodging. Their typical customer is young, health conscious, and from either the United States or Canada. The hotel has experienced low profits despite higher volume and would like for us to determine a cause and potential solution. Is that correct?

Interviewer: **So you're assuming that popularity relates to volume?**

Candidate: I suppose I was, but let me think about that further. I do have one question: Could you please explain to me what constitutes "cabana lodging"?

Interviewer: **"Cabana lodging" is lodging where the guest stays in a small bungalow or house as opposed to a room. This provides the guest with increased privacy and space. What might be a negative aspect of this type of room structure?**

Candidate: I imagine that it's more difficult to manage such rooms as the cleaning team would need to move their equipment from structure to structure. This additional distance would result in more time required to clean, and therefore more money spent on labor.

Interviewer: **Agreed. Please continue.**

Candidate: Excellent, thank you for that clarification. May I have a few moments to collect my thoughts?

Interviewer: **Sure.**

Candidate: We know from the briefing materials that Body Surf Hotel has experienced lower profits. Since revenues and costs drive profitability, I'd like to delve into each of those areas to identify the issue. First, let's look at revenues, which can be split into price and volume. Next, we'll look at costs. This should lead us to the root problem and enable us to brainstorm a few potential solutions. Does this approach sound reasonable?

Interviewer: *That sounds like a logical approach to me. How would you break down costs to better isolate potential issues?*

Candidate: Hmm. I could look at operating costs and financing costs.

Interviewer: *What about costs that remain the same regardless of volume versus costs that are directly affected by volume?*

Candidate: Ah, you're referring to fixed and variable costs.

Interviewer: *Precisely.*

Candidate: Right, so I'll split the costs into those two categories. In fact, let's look at fixed costs to begin. Do we have any information on the company's monthly expenses?

Interviewer: *What are some examples of typical monthly business expenses?*

Candidate: I'm thinking of things like insurance, utilities, and leases.

Interviewer: *Those definitely fall into the standard bucket of monthly expenses. I'd add salaries to the list as well. It just so happens that we have a breakdown of Body Surf Hotel's monthly fixed costs:*

- *salary: $570,000*
- *utilities: $10,000*
- *other: $20,000*

Candidate: Perfect. That comes out to $600,000 in monthly fixed expenses. Has this changed significantly in the last three to five years?

Interviewer: *It has not.*

Candidate: Okay, so we've got stable fixed expenses. How about on the variable side? What is the cost per guest per stay?

Interviewer: *On average, each guest costs about $2,000 per stay. This cost includes transportation to and from the airport, food, cleaning, depreciation of surfing equipment, and T-shirts provided by the company.*

Candidate: And in a typical month, how many guests does Body Surf Hotel receive?

Interviewer: *In the high season, they receive about 200 guests per month. In the low season, the number is closer to 100. High and low season are split equally across the year, six months each.*

Candidate: Wow, so it's a highly cyclical business. Which makes sense when you consider the tourism industry as a whole and outdoor tourist attractions in particular. For example, many European cities are pleasant to visit regardless of the season, while the popularity of ski lodges and beaches are limited to months with favorable weather conditions.

Interviewer: *Good point.*

Candidate: Have the variable expenses changed recently?

Interviewer: *Last year, the company added four extra meals per guest at a cost of $10 per meal.*

Candidate: Okay, so that equals $40 more per guest. Compared to the $2,000 overall cost per guest, the $40 doesn't seem to be a significant increase.

Interviewer: *What percentage increase does the $40 represent?*

Candidate: Let's see . . . 1 percent of $2,000 is $20, so $40 is equal to 2 percent.

Interviewer: *Your math is correct, but technically the increase was $40 added to last year's cost of $1,960. Adding the two gives us our current cost of $2,000. Regardless, I agree that the increase wasn't substantial.*

Candidate: I see, my apologies. Well, since both variable and fixed costs have remained relatively stagnant, let's take a look at our revenue levers, starting with price. What's the price of cabana lodging, what's the price of a surf lesson, and has either price changed recently?

Interviewer: *Body Surf Hotel sells only one product: overnight surf packages priced at $6,000 per person.*

Candidate: Perfect. And concerning volume, we know that the hotel is popular, but is that being translated into more sales?

Interviewer: *Great question. Can you provide me with an example of a popular business not producing sales?*

Candidate: Sure. The first businesses that come to mind are social media websites. Many of these sites don't allow advertisements until long after they're massively popular.

Interviewer: *You chose a relevant example. Body Surf Hotel's popularity is due mainly to the company's social media presence. The company's marketing team produces a creative, entertaining travel blog that has caught on in the amateur surf community. Despite this success, the business has seen a decline in customer purchases each of the past three years.*

Candidate: Interesting. As we noted previously, the surf-lodging market is highly cyclical, so the decline could be a long-term industry fluctuation caused by a macro event such as a North American recession. Given this information, I'd like to learn more about two things. First, we should analyze the skill sets of the owners and employees to see if there might be another product the company could sell during the industry downturn. Second, we should determine if Body Surf Hotel's marketing program could be extended to untapped geographies such as Asia, South America, or Europe. Perhaps these areas haven't been affected by the issues at play in North America. Let's start with skill sets...

Interviewer: *I'm not sure I agree with the assumptions you've made. Can you explain why you're focusing on the macro level?*

Candidate: Well, we've seen that the industry has declined over the past three years.

Interviewer: *I don't believe we ever confirmed the decline was experienced across the entire market.*

Candidate: Ah. That was definitely a quick assumption on my part. Sorry about that. Let's back up a bit. Do we have any information that might help us narrow down the cause of the profitability decline?

Interviewer: *Based on preliminary research, it seems the other local operators have actually increased sales over the same time period.*

Candidate: How do Body Surf Hotel's prices compare to those of competitors in the area?

Interviewer: *The average price for overnight surf hotels with structured activities is $4,000.*

Candidate: Okay, so it's definitely not an industry-wide trend. I think I have all the information I need for now. May I have a few moments to collect my thoughts?

Interviewer: *Of course.*

Candidate: As you can see here on my worksheet, I've listed out what we know so far. With stagnant costs, decreasing volume, highly cyclical tourist seasons, and higher-than-average prices, Body Surf Hotel is struggling to stay profitable. Regardless of season, the company faces $600,000 in fixed costs per month. In terms of variable costs, the hotel experiences costs of $2,000 per customer. By charging a price of $6,000, the hotel is able to earn $4,000 in profit per customer.

Interviewer: *What is that profit margin in percentage terms?*

Candidate: Let's see . . . for each sale, $4,000 in profit divided by $6,000 in price gives us a 66 percent profit margin.

Interviewer: *Perfect, please continue.*

Candidate: So with a profit margin per customer of $4,000, multiplied by 200 customers, Body Surf Hotel earns $800,000 in revenues per month during the high season. This covers the fixed costs of $600,000 and results in $200,000 in profits each month, or $1.2 million per high season.

$4,000 margin
× 200 customers
= $800,000 revenue
− $600,000 fixed cost
= $200,000 profit per month

$200,000 profit
× 6 months
= $1.2 million profit
per high season

During low season, when there are 100 customers per month, Body Surf Hotel earns only $400,000 in monthly revenues, resulting in a net loss of $200,000 per month, or $1.2 million per low season.

$4,000 margin
× 100 customers
= $400,000 revenue
− $600,000 fixed cost
= ($200,000 loss) per month

($200,000 loss)
× 6 months
= $1.2 million loss
per low season

Combining the low and high season, we can see that the company is exactly breakeven.

Interviewer: *I see. Do we know what's driving this?*

Candidate: Based on the competitor data, it seems that Body Surf Hotel's pricing is significantly higher than the other options available to potential customers.

Interviewer: *Can you suggest a way to remedy the issue?*

Candidate: Definitely. Do you mind if I take a few seconds to gather my thoughts?

Interviewer: *Not a problem.*

Candidate: Great. As you can see here in my notes, we began this profitability analysis by reviewing Body Surf Hotel's variable and fixed costs, both of which were found to be relatively stable over the past few years. We then considered the company's revenue, which was stagnant despite overall industry growth. Characterized by a higher-than-average price point, Body Surf Hotel's pricing strategy does little to account for competition and tourism cyclicality.

As a solution to the company's profit issues, I recommend that the company lower its package price to match the industry standard during the low season. This should drive more volume and offset more fixed costs.

Thus, if Body Surf Hotel can increase low season sales volume to an average of 200 guests per month at the price of $5,000 per guest, the company would produce $600,000 each month after variable expenses. After subtracting fixed costs, the company would breakeven throughout the low season, which translates into a $1.2 million annual profit.

$3,000 margin	$0 profit per low season
× 200 customers	+ $1.2 million profit
= $600,000 revenue	per high season
− $600,000 fixed cost	= $1.2 million annual profit
= $0 profit per month	

Interviewer: *That sounds like a major improvement on the company's financials. If we had more time, what else would you want to know to better inform your recommendation?*

Candidate: Given more time, it would be helpful to examine the price elasticity of the surf-lodging packages.

Interviewer: *Do you mind explaining that a bit more? What do you mean by "price elasticity," and how could it assist us in our efforts?*

Candidate: Of course. Currently we're making an assumption about how much sales volume would increase if Body Surf Hotel were to reduce the price of the surf-lodging package. We don't have any data to support this assumption. Given more time, we could test the theory by using a range of prices to determine the exact relationship between price and volume. In other words, we could determine the price elasticity.

Interviewer: *Excellent, thank you. That concludes our case. We've got a few more minutes until our time is up. Do you have any questions for me?*

Candidate: I can't believe I made that industry-wide assumption earlier in the case. In an actual consulting project, how do you avoid making a similar mistake?

Interviewer: *I wouldn't worry about it. You got back on track fairly quickly. But to answer your question, our firm uses both raw data and analyst reports to stay up to date on global trends. This allows us to better contextualize a client's position in a given market, which then . . .*

20 ~~19~~ ~~18~~ ~~17~~ ~~16~~ ~~15~~

14   13   12   11   10   9   8

7   6   5   4   3   2   1

15

Internal/External Framework

You should now understand the basic flow of the case interview. You've navigated two cases and seen how to apply fundamental techniques and the profitability framework.

The second framework to master is the **internal/external framework**. This framework is helpful in cases that involve companies considering or experiencing major changes that require weighing many different options. It allows you to evaluate all aspects of the company, including the environment in which the company operates, to make sound decisions.

You would apply this framework to the following types of cases:

- mergers and acquisitions
- divestiture strategy
- company restructuring
- new product development or launch

- market expansion into new geographies
- supply chain optimization
- building new facilities
- rebranding
- competitive advantage
- government/regulatory environment changes

Notice that this framework is widely applicable. That is its purpose; by focusing broadly, you don't need to memorize 50 specific frameworks for 50 specific case problems. The internal/external framework allows you to organize your thoughts without forcing them to fit into a niche framework.

Internal

Let's start with an example. Your client is Tea Breeze, a beverage company based in Los Angeles, California, that specializes in organic herbal teas, grown locally and sold primarily in the United States and Canada. As a start-up founded within the last two years, Tea Breeze is laser focused on expansion and is considering launching a new product. They hired you to analyze which product would best facilitate a rapid

FIRM PROFILE: BAIN & COMPANY

Bain & Company is one of the world's leading strategy firms, and it has worked with more than two-thirds of the Global 500. The firm stands apart from the competition for its focus on private equity clients and a practice of "tied economics," where the firm often takes equity in lieu of fees. Internally, Bain & Company fosters an entrepreneurial culture, having spun-off successful enterprises such as Bain Capital and The Bridgespan Group. Another distinctive trait is that Bain & Company applies a home-staffing model, which reduces plane travel for consultants. That being said, international opportunities remain for gaining global exposure.

expansion in sales. What questions come to mind when considering the internal factors that may affect a product launch?

- What products does Tea Breeze currently sell?
- Do they grow their own tea, or do they outsource production?
- What type of ownership structure is in place, and who has decision rights on the type of new product they launch?
- Do they have any preconceived notions about the type of product they will launch?
- Do their employees have the skill sets to produce, market, and sell beverages other than tea?
- What types of technology and facilities are required to launch a new product?

With little information in the case prompt, an endless number of questions come to mind. When evaluating the internal aspects of the case, start by addressing four buckets:

- people
- product
- process
- technology

People are the owners, employees, and stakeholders of a company. Typical questions for consideration may include: What is the ownership structure? Is it a public or private company? Is it backed by private equity or a venture capital group? Who has decision rights? Who are the employees? What are their levels of expertise and skill sets? Are they geographically spread out, or are they based in one region? What other stakeholders must be taken into consideration?

Product refers to the goods or services that a company sells. Questions for consideration may include: What does the company sell? What is their price point? How diverse is their product portfolio? Is there potential for cannibalization between products (i.e., are they creating internal competition between two or more products)? Are products sold online, in-store, or both?

"After hearing about the pressure of the case interview, I expected my experience would be intimidating and stressful. I was relieved to see that each and every one of my interviewers wanted me to succeed. You may make mistakes that seem critical in the moment, but ultimately the interviewer wants to see how well you adapt and keep pushing forward in a logical and engaging way. When I was matched up with a partner and senior manager during my final round at Deloitte, I tripped up at a couple of points but focused on getting back on track. Preparing beforehand significantly reduced my stress on interview day. I recommend giving and practicing a good number of case interviews with your friends in the three to four weeks leading up to your interview. In time, you will get a feel for both sides of the interview and be more comfortable with whatever case gets thrown at you!"

Geoff G., Consultant, Deloitte

Process is the protocols and procedures a company uses to maintain daily operations. Questions to ask may include: How efficiently does the company operate? Do they make their products or outsource production? Are they optimized across the supply chain, from manufacturing to distribution to point of sale? Do they have proper quality control standards in place? Do they follow specific regulatory codes?

Technology refers to the systems and platforms on which a company operates. It also encompasses how a company gathers and stores data. Questions to pose during the case interview may include: How integrated are technology systems within the business? How well does the company gather and use data on its customers? Are its systems out of date? Does technology inhibit the company from operating efficiently? How much does technology cost the business?

Considerations will vary based on the type of case. A bank will operate much differently than a clothing retailer or an integrated energy firm.

However, if you focus on people, product, process, and technology, you'll gain a deep understanding of the internal factors at play and, consequently, you'll be able to zoom in quickly on potential solutions.

External

Understanding the company in a vacuum won't necessarily lead you to a solution. For a more complete picture, you need to learn about the external environment in which the company operates. For example, let's reconsider your client, Tea Breeze. Let's say you evaluated all the internal factors associated with Tea Breeze's new product launch and determined that they should expand by launching a new herbal energy drink. What if its customers are health buffs and oppose the concept of energy drinks? What if the energy drink market in the United States and Canada has declined in the last two years? What if 3 energy drinks already dominate 75 percent of the market? What if 20 new competitors entered the market in the past year? What if the FDA has placed heavy regulations on energy drinks?

You can't make sound decisions without understanding the external factors that may affect the outcome. When evaluating the external environment, focus on four buckets:

- customers
- market
- competitors
- risks

FACTOID

McKinsey & Company is partially responsible for popularizing the barcode among retail businesses. In 1973, the firm organized a consortium of grocery chains to reach an agreement on how to implement the nascent technology to realize cost savings and better study customer behaviors.

Customers are the buyers of a company's products. Customers may be individual consumers or other businesses. When considering customers, you may want to determine their demographics, preferences, and buying habits. What is their age range, geographical location, and income level? What do they like? How frequently do they buy? How many customers are repeat buyers?

Market refers to the overall landscape of products or services. When evaluating the marketplace, it's important to inquire about size, proportions, and trends. How big is the market in dollar terms? What is the size of the user base? Is it saturated? Is it highly fragmented or dominated by a few players? Is it growing, or is it shrinking? How easy is it to enter? What are the barriers to entry? Is there any cyclicality, seasonality, or regular sales fluctuation? Think of the market like a pie. Each company involved gets a piece of the pie in varying proportions. Some pies are big, some are small, some are tough to cut into, and some are just plain stale.

Competitors are other companies or organizations that offer similar products or services, and thus may take business away from your client. It's important to gain a deep understanding of competition. Who are your key competitors? How many competitors are there? What portion of the market do they occupy? What are their prices? Do they specialize in a niche, or do they operate more broadly? Are there emerging competitors that the industry hasn't been monitoring? An example of this last case would be the recent foray into self-driving cars made by giant tech companies. The auto industry likely didn't see that curveball coming.

MYTH: I WILL BOTHER A CONSULTANT IF I SEND THEM A NETWORKING EMAIL.

Consultants enjoy receiving emails from recruits. Take time to draft a thoughtful, succinct note. If requesting a meeting, always accommodate their schedule first. Also, send a follow-up note to thank them for their time.

Finally, consider **risks**, or the environmental factors that may threaten a particular outcome. Risks are heavily dependent on the case. Potential considerations may include regulations, laws, geographic concerns, and cultural considerations. Risks are helpful to discuss near the end of the case to ensure you haven't missed any critical data.

Tomorrow, you will conduct your third mock case interview. See if you can apply either the profitability framework or the internal/external framework to organize your thoughts and arrive at a solution.

LEARNING TARGETS:

◎ *Master the application of the internal/external framework to a wide variety of cases such as mergers and acquisitions and supply chain optimization.*

◎ *Consider all the internal aspects of a case (people, product, process, technology), as well as the external aspects (customers, market, competitors, risks).*

CASE INTERVIEW IN

14

DAYS

Mock Interview No. 3

Read through the following script with a friend or classmate. Next, review the instructions for live case practice on page 166. When ready, have your partner use the interview guide on page 169 to lead you through the case as if it were an actual interview.

Interviewer: *Swirl Tech Inc. is a medical device company based in Seattle, Washington. They manage the product development process from alpha testing all the way to mass commercial production. The company's core product line specializes in devices that produce a virtual overlay of various measurements and data that surgeons can use while looking through a microscope. Similar to the displays currently used in fighter jets and luxury automobiles, the additional data reduces the need to look away from the patient and therefore dramatically reduces the incidence of human error during a given procedure. Swirl Tech is in the final stages of developing a new generation of its product. Due to its cutting-edge nature, the product is* *projected to generate strong sales. Swirl Tech has asked for your help to determine when they should launch the product.*

Candidate: May I have a minute to organize my thoughts?

Interviewer: *Sure thing.*

Candidate: Okay, I'm going to repeat the information we know to make sure I didn't miss anything. Our client is Swirl Tech Inc., a medical device company based in the American Northwest. Their most recently developed product allows for a virtual overlay of information on a microscope lens that helps doctors avoid making errors during surgery. The client plans to launch the product but is unsure about the exact timing. They've enlisted our help to resolve the matter. Does that sound right?

Interviewer: *I believe that's everything.*

Candidate: Great. May I have a few moments to think about the next steps?

Interviewer: *Of course.*

Candidate: Based on what we know, it doesn't seem that profitability is necessarily the key driver in making a decision on launch timing. Therefore, I'd like to start with a more macro approach that will allow us to quickly get down to the main considerations. From a high level, I'd like to consider internal and external factors related to the company. On the internal side, I'll focus on our client's background and products so we can better understand any preexisting plans for the launch. Externally, I'll cover the customers, lens device market, competitors, and risks. Analyzing the customers and market conditions will give us better context, while reviewing competitors will reveal the level of urgency to launch. Finally, explicitly targeting risks will help uncover the concerns that led Swirl Tech to ask for our help.

Interviewer: *Interesting. I like the thorough approach. Let's see where it takes us.*

Candidate: Excellent. Starting with the client, what is Swirl Tech's ownership structure?

Interviewer: *What are some examples of ownership structure, and why is this important?*

Candidate: A company can either be publicly or privately owned. Ownership typically defines the timeline and approach a company takes toward product development and launch. If the company is public, it's more likely to be held accountable by investors, who demand that products be produced and launched in a profitable, timely manner. If the company is privately owned, the launch timing and profitability aspects may be less important. However, with less public oversight, product-quality standards may drop as well. Finally, if the company is owned by an aggressive investor, such as a venture capital firm, it's likely that a short timeline would be of utmost importance to ensure that the investors get their money back quickly.

Interviewer: *For the most part, I agree with those generalizations. It turns out that Swirl Tech is venture backed.*

Candidate: Ok, so there may be a high sense of urgency. Concerning the product, is this the first version or has Swirl Tech launched similar products in the past?

Interviewer: *This version represents the third generation.*

Candidate: What was the timing of past launches? How long does it take Swirl Tech to take a product from inception to commercialization?

Interviewer: *Development on the first project began four years ago. Each new generation has taken about two years to develop and sell commercially.*

Candidate: What was the market's response to the first two generations?

Interviewer: *The first wasn't adopted quickly and had a high failure rate, leading to frustrated surgeons and high replacement costs for Swirl Tech. Major improvements were made in the second generation, and sales doubled over the course of two years. This third product takes an even bigger step toward customization and* *sophistication. However, so far there has been limited time to solicit feedback from KOLs.*

Candidate: I'm sorry, I'm not familiar with that term. What exactly is a KOL?

Interviewer: *Key Opinion Leader. In the life sciences industry, KOLs are top doctors that team with companies to help develop better products. They use their expertise to expose flaws in a product they're testing, and then help market the product once it meets the doctors' expectations. For these services, the KOLs are paid a substantial amount by companies, given steep discounts, and granted first access to new products.*

Candidate: Wow, sounds like a good gig. I think I've got a good sense now about internal considerations. Let's shift to external factors, starting with customers. Aside from doctors, who else buys the device?

Interviewer: *Who do you think might buy it?*

Candidate: Uh … I'm not sure … I honestly don't know anything about the industry.

Interviewer: *Just take a guess.*

Candidate: Hmm … perhaps there are other professionals, such as biologists, who might find uses for the virtual overlay of information?

Interviewer: *I love the creativity, but in this case it's actually medical clinics and hospitals that purchase equipment. About 50 percent of Swirl Tech's sales are to physicians and 50 percent to hospitals and clinics.*

Candidate: Okay, that's helpful to know. Regarding the market, do we know if it's been growing or declining over the past three to five years?

Interviewer: *The market has been mostly stagnant in the United States due to high saturation of more basic versions of the product, but it's growing in nearly every other geography.*

Candidate: Got it. You mentioned other, more basic versions. Let's change gears to focus more on competitors. Who is Swirl Tech competing with?

Interviewer: *There is one other major player that makes less sophisticated virtual overlays. That company recently made large investments in research and development, and they're presumed to have the capability to create a comparably advanced product within the next 24 months.*

Candidate: Interesting. So to recap, let's walk through the summary slides I've sketched here on my notepad. We've got a venture-backed firm whose new product has a temporary technical advantage over the competitor's, but it also has a checkered history with high product-failure rates, followed by a higher quality product with stronger growth potential. The new version is significantly more sophisticated than the last, but it has had limited field testing with KOLs.

Interviewer: *That sounds right to me.*

Candidate: My initial hypothesis is that the product may not be ready for launch quite yet. It seems like there are too many moving parts. Let's dig deeper on potential risks. What main risks has Swirl Tech identified in relation to the launch?

Interviewer: *I think you may already know. Can you list a few risks based on what you've learned so far, and what the implications of those risks might be?*

Candidate: That's fair. If you don't mind, I'm going to take a few seconds to jot down my thoughts.

Interviewer: *Of course.*

Candidate: Okay, from what we know, there are two core risks related to the launch. First, there's the risk that the product isn't ready, thus tarnishing the company's reputation, causing expensive repairs, and further delaying investors' returns. We know this has happened to

Swirl Tech before, so we'll want to pay extra attention to this possibility. Second, there's the risk that Swirl Tech's main competitor will launch a similar product before Swirl Tech does, which would affect Swirl Tech's sales potential, market prestige, and the respect it earns from its KOLs.

Interviewer: *Correct. What else would you like to know?*

Candidate: At what stage of development is the newest product?

Interviewer: *It is about 90 percent complete and has been in development and testing for a little under a year.*

Candidate: Wow, so Swirl Tech is compacting this project's timeline so that it's much shorter than the two-year average seen with the first two generations. With up to 24 months remaining until the competitor creates a similar product, it seems like Swirl Tech could safely take some additional time to ensure all quality standards have been met. But we need to quantify the risk versus reward. On the reward side, we need to know what Swirl Tech has estimated for sales, using the initial project start date as a baseline. In fact, we need to know their sales projections for three different scenarios: if they were to launch the product one year after the project start date, two years after, and three years after.

Interviewer: *The product is priced at $60,000. The estimated unit sales for product launches in one, two, and three years are 500, 400, and 200, respectively.*

Candidate: So that translates to $300 million, $240 million, and $120 million in revenue.

Interviewer: *You may be off by a zero.*

Candidate: Ah, thanks, I meant $30 million, $24 million, and $12 million. What's the estimated cost of replacement parts if the medical device experiences high failure rates?

Interviewer: *Can you tell me another cost that might be associated with a product with high rates of failure?*

Candidate: If the product wasn't performing as advertised, I imagine the company would experience lower interest from its customer base, which would result in lower sales.

Interviewer: *Good. Let's group replacement parts and sales loss together for ease of calculation. A 0.5 percent rate of failure would result in $2 million in costs, a 2 percent rate would result in $12 million, and 5 percent would result in $25 million.*

Candidate: Got it. Finally, is there a correlation between length of development timeline and a given failure rate?

Interviewer: *There's a 3-year development period for a 0.5 percent failure rate, 2 years for 2 percent, and 1 year for 5 percent.*

Candidate: I think that's all the information I need. May I take a moment to run some numbers?

Interviewer: *Of course, just be sure to talk me through your calculations once you're ready.*

Candidate: Okay, as you can see in the slides I've sketched, we began this analysis by considering the effect of Swirl Tech's venture capital–ownership structure, as well as its previous product launch timelines. After receiving further information on launch risks, such as low-quality products and the cost of replacements, it seems that we have three options to consider for the launch, with each resulting in a different level of profitability.

Launch after 1 year of development:	$30 million – $25 million = $5 million profit
Launch after 2 years:	$24 million – $12 million = $12 million profit
Launch after 3 years:	$12 million – $2 million = $10 million profit

Based on these calculations, it seems that launching two years after development is the most profitable option. There are three important reasons why Swirl Tech should delay the launch of their product for at least one more year: maximize quality, reduce failure rates, and increase financial gains.

Interviewer: *Fantastic. What might be some additional considerations that would influence Swirl Tech to delay the product launch?*

Candidate: I imagine that Swirl Tech's position as a venture-backed company would make it difficult to further delay the launch. However, the investors are more likely to realize solid gains if Swirl Tech is able to foster its image as a quality-focused company. Moreover, extra time could allow for additional enhancements, more robust marketing, and further circulation of the device among KOLs.

Interviewer: *I agree, and I'm glad you provided both financial and strategic reasons for your recommendation. This concludes our case, thank you. Any questions for me?*

Candidate: If this was an actual client, what ended up happening?

Interviewer: *This example is actually fictional, though I've seen this "launch now" versus "launch later" debate arise many times in my career. Typically, we see a result similar to the one you recommended. In fact, just last year ...*

13

Categorize and Group

You've completed one-third of your case interview boot camp. While you may be feeling nervous as the interview date approaches, remind yourself that you're taking the steps necessary to walk into your interview in two weeks with confidence and poise.

Over the past week, we've focused on case interview fundamentals and two frameworks: profitability and internal/external. The good news is these two structures apply to nearly 99 percent of cases. You don't need to memorize 50 arbitrary frameworks (e.g., Porter's Five Forces, The Four Cs) to understand fundamental business concepts and use full cognition during the case interview. While niche frameworks may help expand your business acumen, trying to memorize them all will only confuse you on interview day. Further, you run a higher risk of trying to force the case to fit a specific framework.

It's time to shift gears and learn about techniques for organizing your thoughts as you move deeper into the case. In this chapter, we will discuss an important organizational technique called categorize and group.

Most cases are not cut-and-dry. You will rarely get a case that is only focused on one concept or goal. Depending on the level of difficulty, many cases will require you to examine two or more business challenges. This may require more than one framework. You should categorize the different focus areas and group your logical reasoning into those categories.

Case Study: Love Me, Please

Let's say your client is a dating website called Love Me, Please, which launched before more popular, mobile dating applications came on the scene. Since then, your client's revenue has been declining, despite the fact that their online competitors' sales have remained steady. In this case, what would you focus on? Clearly, there is a revenue issue. However, the competitive landscape appears to be a bit complicated as well. Instead of examining only one thread, you may want to focus on multiple areas, such as:

- client's volume trends
- client's price trends
- competitors' pricing
- client's product positioning versus the market

These focus areas fit both of our fundamental frameworks. That's okay. A common mistake that candidates make during the case interview is attempting to force-fit a case into one framework. While frameworks are intended to provide structure during the case, you should also be

MYTH: YOU CAN'T HAVE A FAMILY AS A CONSULTANT.

Work/life balance is a challenge in any profession, including consulting. Your spouse may do the heavy lifting for parenting during the week, so try to alleviate his or her responsibilities when you're home.

flexible enough to think outside your framework. As a general rule, fit the framework to the case; don't fit the case to the framework.

Without confusing yourself or your interviewer, how should you go about examining multiple focus areas? First, establish an approach. No consultant begins a client engagement without developing a plan, and your interviewers expect no less of you during the case interview. While sitting in silence for 30 to 60 seconds may seem awkward, the extra time will demonstrate your ability to think calmly and logically under pressure.

To come up with an approach, categorize your focus areas and then group your steps of logical reasoning. For Love Me, Please, let's use two categories: revenue and marketplace. Next, let's outline an approach for examining the categories systematically. In the interview, verbally walk your interviewer through your approach and rationale.

"Given the information at hand, I'd like to start by examining my client's volume and price trends. Second, I'd like to take a deeper look into competitor pricing and product positioning. By assessing Love Me, Please's revenue drivers, I can identify potential trends in pricing or volume that are driving down sales revenue. Combining this information with competitor pricing and product positioning in the marketplace, I should get a better idea of why their direct, online competitors have been less affected by the entry of new dating applications."

Categorizing and grouping information allows you to isolate variables. Think back to high school algebra. Say you have two variables, x and y, and an equation, $34y^2 = 25x + 500$. To solve for either variable, you need a second equation, such as $5x = 405$. To solve for y, you must first solve for x, plug it into the equation, and then isolate the variable y. After you've isolated each variable, you can see both solutions as a whole picture. The same logic follows for the case interview. To solve for revenue and marketplace, you must first isolate the variables within revenue, then marketplace, and then view the whole picture in aggregate.

First, let's look at revenue. You learn that Love Me, Please hasn't updated their prices in the past two years. You then confirm with your interviewer that, in fact, volume is an issue—it has decreased by more than 20 percent each year. Does pricing account for the decrease in volume? We can't answer that question until we examine the second category: marketplace.

Start by inquiring about competitor pricing. How do more popular online competitors' prices compare to our client's? You learn that each company charges a premium membership fee, while Love Me, Please does not charge a membership fee. This seems odd. Shouldn't higher prices mean that customers would leave competitors' websites for our client's more affordable option? As it turns out, there is another variable to isolate within this category: product positioning.

Finally, you inquire about product positioning and learn that Love Me, Please has targeted a younger customer base: people 18 to 25 years old who are looking for casual relationships. Alternatively, other online

---

FACTOID

Bain & Company was one of the first firms to accept equity in lieu of charging fees. Moreover, Bain led the charge toward value-based billing, where the consulting firm receives a percentage of the benefits earned through client engagement. This structure provides the consulting firm with more upside and limits downside risk for the client.

CASE INTERVIEW DON'TS

There are plenty of ways to be successful on interview day, especially when you've prepared rigorously. The competitive nature of the consulting interview process, however, leaves little margin for error. To avoid falling into common traps, below are the top 10 "don'ts" for interview day.

DON'T BE LATE. Show up to your interview at least 30 minutes early to be safe. Not only is it rude and unprofessional to be late, but it also wastes your interviewer's valuable time. Unless you experience an emergency on interview day, tardiness is almost a guaranteed deal breaker.

DON'T TREAT YOUR COMPETITION LIKE COMPETITION. Someday the person sitting next to you in the waiting room may be your coworker. Be friendly. Make small talk. You're all in this together. Show the consulting greeters that you're at ease and confident. It will be noted.

DON'T NAME DROP. Perceived arrogance is an easy way to turn off your interviewer. Unless you're bonding over a mutual friend, name dropping tends to be viewed negatively. Avoid boisterous reunions or high fives with friends you may have at the firm. It's important to be humble and gracious on interview day.

DON'T HIGHLIGHT YOUR WEAKNESSES. Know and play to your strengths. Don't dwell on your weaknesses. While your interviewer may address holes in your résumé, such as a low GPA or ACT score, or lack of internship experience, don't highlight your weaknesses unsolicited. For example, your interviewer doesn't need to know if you're inexperienced with data analytics or weak at mental math.

DON'T DISCUSS OTHER FIRMS. Your interviewer and peers don't need to know where else you're interviewing. Conversing about other firms, positively or negatively, is inappropriate in an interview setting. Consulting is a small world, and it's easy to offend people by gossiping about people at other firms.

DON'T POST INCRIMINATING PHOTOS ON SOCIAL MEDIA. There's a strong chance that someone from the firm will review your social media sites. Take down any pictures you wouldn't be comfortable showing to your grandmother.

DON'T PANIC. You can make mistakes during the case interview and still get hired. Just take a deep breath and move on.

DON'T BE AFRAID TO ASK QUESTIONS. Remember, interviewing is a two-way street. You need to determine if the job is right for you as well. Ask probing, honest questions to make sure you leave your interview with very little uncertainty.

DON'T DISCUSS THE CASE OUTSIDE YOUR INTERVIEW. Typically, candidates interview in shifts. Your interview may be before someone else's. It's inappropriate to discuss the case's content or difficulty level before someone else has interviewed. Further, you don't want your interviewer to overhear you whining that you bombed the case, or worse, bragging that you nailed it.

DON'T FORGET TO SEND A THANK-YOU NOTE. Thank-you notes are important for two reasons: they show your interviewer gratitude for their time and consideration, and they are an ideal way for you to stay in the mind of the person who interviewed you. Remember, the interviewer may have seen several people before and after interviewing you. Send a note between 30 minutes and 3 hours after your interview.

competitors position their products for an older crowd: people who are between 30 and 50 years old and are looking for serious, long-term relationships. Bingo. By isolating the variables, you learn that our client, unlike its online competitors, is directly competing with new dating apps, which position their products to the same customer base. You can infer that the dating apps are stealing market share from our client, and then go on to make recommendations around product positioning.

While a multifaceted case may seem daunting at first, isolating the variables by categorizing and grouping them can make the solution much clearer.

LEARNING TARGETS:

◎ *Fit the framework to the case, not the case to the framework.*

◎ *When you have a case with multiple focal points, categorize your focus areas and then group your steps of logical reasoning. This approach will allow you to isolate variables.*

12

DAYS

Mock Interview No. 4

Read through the following script with a friend or classmate. Next, review the instructions for live case practice on page 166. When ready, have your partner use the interview guide on page 171 to lead you through the case as if it were an actual interview.

Interviewer: *Aussie Alpine is a ski resort tucked away in the mountains of southeastern Australia. Boasting a multitude of slope styles, terrain parks, ski shops, restaurants, condos, and retail outlets, Aussie Alpine leads the national ski resort market in revenue, producing $350 million in total sales each year. Despite its market dominance, the company has experienced stagnant top-line growth, and its leadership team is growing concerned that competitors may soon catch up. Our consulting firm has been hired to identify a remedy for Aussie Alpine's growth issues.*

Candidate: May I have a minute to organize my thoughts?

Interviewer: *Sure thing.*

Candidate: If you don't mind, I'd like to repeat the details you just provided to verify I haven't missed anything. I understand that the client is Aussie Alpine, an Australian ski resort that dominates the market but is experiencing growth issues. The company has a diverse set of revenue streams, including ski slopes, restaurants, shops, and lodging. Combined, these assets produce $350 million in total sales per year. Does that sound right?

Interviewer: *That's correct.*

Candidate: Great. I do have one question: can you please provide more details on Aussie Alpine's market position? I just want to be clear on what exactly constitutes "market dominance."

Interviewer: *Good point. I don't have exact information on Aussie Alpine's market position, but how would you go about determining the value of the overall market?*

Candidate: Since we weren't given that information, we'll have to calculate it. To value the market, we need to know two things. First, how many people visit a ski resort in Australia each year? Second, how much on average does the typical guest spend while at an Australian ski resort?

Interviewer: *I agree with that approach and happen to have information along those lines. The Australian ski market consists of about 2.1 million skier visits annually. The average skier visit produces $308 of revenue.*

Candidate: Got it. Do you mind if I round $308 to $300 for the sake of simplicity?

Interviewer: *No problem.*

Candidate: In terms of annual revenue, $300 per person multiplied by 2.1 million visits equates to $630 million. In other words, our total market size is $630 million.

Interviewer: *Based on what we know, how many visits does Aussie Alpine receive, and what is their market share in percentage terms?*

Candidate: Let's see, we'll take $350 million in Aussie Alpine sales and divide it by $630 million total market size. We can quickly calculate that 50 percent of $630 million is $315 million. So the client's sales are larger than 50 percent but not quite 60 percent of the market. Let's say Aussie Alpine has roughly 55 percent market share.

Changing gears to the number of skiers who visit, we need to know 55 percent of the 2.1 million total. So, 50 percent of 2.1 million visits is 1.05 million. Five percent is 0.105 million visits. So adding those together, 55 percent is roughly 1.2 million skier visits to Aussie Alpine.

0.50 × $630 million total market sales = $315 million sales	0.50 × 2.1 million total visits = 1.05 million skier visits
0.05 × $630 million total market sales = $31.5 million sales	0.05 x 2.1 million total visits = 0.105 million skier visits
$315 million + $31.5 million = $346.5 million	1.05 million + 0.105 million = ~1.2 million skier visits to Aussie Alpine
Aussie Alpine sales = ~55% market share	

Interviewer: *Nice work. Let's continue with the case.*

Candidate: Excellent. Can I take a few minutes to determine my approach?

Interviewer: *No problem.*

Candidate: Based on what we know so far, I'm interpreting the term "growth issues" to be a signal that Aussie Alpine is experiencing revenue-related problems. To dig a bit deeper, I'd like to break revenue into two components: price and volume.

Interviewer: *That sounds reasonable to me.*

Candidate: Starting with price, has Aussie Alpine changed its pricing structure in the last three to five years?

Interviewer: *Prices have remained level over that time period.*

Candidate: How do these prices compare with competitors?

Interviewer: *Aussie Alpine is a high-volume resort because they maintain more affordable prices than other operators in the area. Unfortunately, the prices used at the various retail outlets at Aussie Alpine can't be lowered any further from their current positions. Otherwise, the company would become cash-flow negative.*

Candidate: Does that include prices for things like food, alcohol, clothing, and ski lessons?

Interviewer: *It does.*

Candidate: Interesting. Based on Aussie Alpine's marketing position, it sounds like its customer base would be opposed to any substantial price raises. Let's take a look at volume. Concerning skier visits, what has been the trend over the last three to five years?

Interviewer: *The park overall has seen a steady flow of visitors over the past several years, with an average annual growth rate in the low single digits. This trend has echoed throughout the various park outlets as well.*

Candidate: What about Aussie Alpine's overall market share? Has the market grown while our client's sales remained stagnant?

Interviewer: *The Australian ski market is fully saturated and has remained steady as well.*

Candidate: In summary, our client is experiencing stagnant revenue growth. To further complicate the matter, the client has limited ability to adjust prices to increase volume due to profitability concerns and customer expectations. Finally, the ski market overall isn't growing. Given these constraints, we need to find a more creative solution to the growth problem. For example, we could consider ways to increase the quality of the products and services to drive more volume without changing price. Or we could consider expanding our product offerings.

Interviewer: *I like both ideas. How would you approach those considerations?*

Candidate: Aussie Alpine already has a wide range of products that cover the standard ski resort needs. Perhaps if they incorporated other winter sports, such as skimobiles or ice-skating, they could increase revenues.

Interviewer: *Interesting approach. When do you anticipate the client will earn its revenues?*

Candidate: During the winter months, most likely late November through early March.

Interviewer: *Don't forget that Australia is in the Southern Hemisphere.*

Candidate: Ah, right. So perhaps April to September would be their busy months. I see what you're driving toward. What does Aussie Alpine do during the summer months?

Interviewer: *During that period, the company focuses on repairing, rebuilding, or expanding their current assets. The restaurants, bars, and condos at the mountain's base remain open for business. Retail stores are closed for the summer season, as are the slopes, hotels, and the single summit restaurant.*

Candidate: That's our opportunity. Do you mind if I take a moment to brainstorm a few ideas?

Interviewer: *Go right ahead.*

Candidate: Okay, there are four new product offerings I would like for Aussie Alpine to consider. Each would take advantage of what currently is an under-utilized asset. First, the client could build downhill–mountain bike courses on the slopes and host competitions or trainings. Second, they could set up a family-friendly zip-line course. Third, they could open the summit restaurant and hotels for special events such as weddings, banquets, and corporate events. Finally, the resort could build a golf course along the gentler slopes.

Interviewer: *I like the diversity of options, but they sound expensive and timely. How about we try to narrow it down to two suggestions. Of the four, which options require the largest amount of capital? Which will take the longest?*

Candidate: Both the golf and zip-line courses would require substantial investments in time and capital. The golf project would involve redesigning, enhancing, and maintaining massive amounts of land. A zip-line course has less focus on land but still requires the infrastructure of cables and towers. Given this, the options I would focus on are biking and events. Each leverages the assets available and should be relatively easy to implement. This means more dollars, more quickly.

Interviewer: *Excellent, I agree with those choices as well. Let's dig a bit deeper into the event-hosting option. Can you provide the client with an estimate of how much revenue this might earn during the low season?*

Candidate: Sure. Do we have any financial data for the summit restaurant during the ski season? In particular, do we have any information on events currently being held at these locations?

Interviewer: *Let's assume that during the winter, ski customers use the summit restaurant from dawn until dusk each day, leaving no time available for event hosting. The lodging and restaurant facilities can operate at a maximum capacity of 500 people.*

Candidate: Okay. To calculate the revenue opportunity, we need to know price per event attendee and the number of events held during the summer season. From my previous experiences, I estimate that a reasonable daily price per event attendee could be about $1,000 per person, including food, drinks, and lodging. That means that our client could generate $500,000 in revenue from events for every night that the facilities are full. Earlier we said that there were six winter months, so we'll assume that we have six summer months to host events. We'll also assume that the entire venue is reserved 50 percent of the time, 15 nights per month.

To summarize, that's $500,000 multiplied by 15 nights multiplied by six months. In this scenario, Aussie Alpine stands to produce $4.5 million in additional revenue each summer season.

Interviewer: **What does that amount represent in revenue growth for our client?**

Candidate: Let's see, $4.5 million divided by $350 million gives us between 1 percent and 2 percent revenue growth.

Interviewer: **What do you think of that number?**

Candidate: It's not nearly as high as I had hoped it would be, even after using fairly aggressive assumptions. While it is a "quick win" for the client, a 2 percent increase in sales isn't enough to really move the needle. They'll need to consider additional options to meet their revenue goals.

Interviewer: **That's a fair assessment. Let's see what our revenues might be if Aussie Alpine incorporated your biking idea. Again, the client has little relevant data to share on the topic.**

Candidate: No problem. To estimate the revenue opportunity, we need to know the pricing and volume of guests. Let's assume that the standard amount of money spent on a one-day bike pass is $50. We know that there are 2.1 million ski visitors to Aussie Alpine each year.

Interviewer: **Do we?**

Candidate: Ah, my mistake, that was the total market. Aussie Alpine brings in 1.2 million ski visits annually. Given that this population is presumably active and loves the outdoors, let's assume that we can convince 20 percent of those customers to return in the summer to bike. That gives us 240,000 guests over the six summer months. If each person spends $50 on a bike pass, that results in an additional $12 million in revenue per year. Compared to the client's $350 million in total sales, the $12 million biking revenue represents roughly 3 percent or 4 percent revenue growth.

1.2 million ski visits	$12 million biking revenue
× 0.20	÷ $350 million total revenue
= 240,000 biking clients	= ~3 to 4% revenue growth
240,000 biking clients	
× $50 bike pass	
= $12 million biking revenue	

Interviewer: *Based on what we've learned, do you have a recommendation for Aussie Alpine?*

Candidate: I do. May I have a few moments to gather my notes?

Interviewer: *Of course.*

Candidate: Right. As you can see here in my notes, we began this growth analysis by calculating Aussie Alpine's position relative to the overall Australian ski market. Having learned that our client has minimal flexibility to adjust prices, we determined that the company should consider using the summer months as a source of additional revenue. Specifically, by combining biking and event-hosting revenues, we identified between 4 and 6 percent revenue growth opportunities for the company. I would argue that this is a conservative estimate since we haven't taken into consideration the potential for side revenues, such as gift shop sales or nightly pub sales, which are likely to grow with the increased summer traffic.

As such, I recommend that Aussie Alpine create these new business lines. In the stagnant ski industry, the additional growth will propel Aussie Alpine past its competitors and potentially lead to additional off-season opportunities.

Interviewer: *Perfect. Finally, how might the creation of a new summer season affect winter sales?*

Candidate: I expect that the additional summer activity would boost winter sales for two reasons. First, the client could package winter and summer activities into annual passes, thereby driving consumer loyalty. Second, by focusing on non-skiers during the summer months, the client may be able to reach new winter clients or even poach clients from its competitors.

Interviewer: *Well said. That is the end of our case. I'm sure you've received plenty of information on our firm by now, but let me know if you have any questions.*

Candidate: Thank you. I do have one question. This case was a lot of fun, and I loved the creative approach we took. If you were to describe your typical client engagement team, would you say that this type of thought process is common?

Interviewer: *Great question. Without a doubt, I'm constantly amazed at my colleagues' creativity. In consulting, you work with the most brilliant minds in the world. At our firm in particular, you'll find that . . .*

11

The Truth Lies in the Middle

During the four mock interviews you've practiced to date, you explored various industries and geographies. You played with heavy machinery at BullDoze, enjoyed the beaches of Body Surf Hotel, examined medical devices with Swirl Tech, and skied the mountains at Aussie Alpine. You explored profitability challenges, internal and external forces that affect a company's performance, and ways of organizing your thoughts to successfully navigate a case. You also used basic skills, like combining intuition and reasoning, to walk your interviewer step by step through your strategy as you brainstormed creative and logical solutions.

This chapter's lesson will demonstrate how using friendly round numbers and moderate predictions will benefit you during the case interview.

Friendly Numbers

In some case interviews, you will get lucky and be given all the numbers you need to solve the case. Other times, you won't be so lucky and the numbers provided will be tricky to manipulate. In these instances, the key to solving quantitative questions is to use friendly numbers.

Friendly numbers are exactly what they sound like: round, even, easy-to-manipulate integers (e.g., 10; 500; 2,000,000).

The purpose of the case interview is not to test how skilled you are at simple math. Instead, the case is meant to assess how you think and solve problems under pressure. Therefore, make the math as easy as possible so that it doesn't hinder you from organizing and communicating your thoughts.

In the absence of data, you can make the math easy by picking your own friendly numbers. When given data, you can reduce complexity by rounding the numbers to more manageable figures. For example, instead of working with the given price of $97 to solve the case, round it to $100. If provided a revenue of $7.3 billion, adjust the number to $7 billion. Just be sure to confirm with your interviewer that your rounding is

MY INTERVIEW STORY

"Because I attended an undergraduate university without on-campus management consulting recruitment, my interview process was slightly different than the average candidate's experience. Preparing for the 'fit' portion of consulting interviews was particularly important for me, because I had to explain during coffee chats and introductory phone calls why I would make a good consultant before I could even approach a first-round interview. Once an official interview was scheduled, performing well was essential because I never knew if I would get another interview opportunity. Nailing every encounter with consulting practitioners is critical for students from nontarget universities who want to maximize their chances of breaking into consulting."

Business Analyst, Deloitte

acceptable before working on the problem, and don't forget to use words like "about" when providing your rounded solution.

You've already had, and will continue to have, the chance to practice picking and rounding to friendly numbers with your mock interviews. However, many candidates still flounder during quantitative sections because they get tripped up by simple math. Most firms don't allow candidates to bring a calculator into the interview. With that in mind, avoid making silly quantitative mistakes during the interview by freshening up on math skills. You will need to be able to quickly add, subtract, multiply, and divide. You may also need to convert easy percentages to fractions and vice versa. Make yourself flash cards with phrases similar to the following:

- What is 80 percent of $8 billion in revenue?
- What percentage is $12 million of $96 million in profits?
- What is the new price if the current price of $15 is raised by 40 percent?
- What is 30 percent of $700 million in variable expenses?

Relatively simple math becomes confusing when you're stressed and under pressure. The more comfortable you are with manipulating numbers in your head, the fewer careless math mistakes you will make during the interview. However, it's okay to write out your calculations if the problem seems too difficult to do in your head. Better to be slow and correct than fast and wrong.

It also may be helpful to study and memorize a few key population sizes that will serve as reference points. You might be surprised at how many case interviewers ask for your best guess at these figures:

- world population: 7 billion
- United States population: 300 million
- China population: 1 billion
- India population: 1 billion
- New York City population: 10 million

You probably noticed that all of the populations are rounded. You don't need to know exact numbers during the interview. Remember, the focus is to use reasonable, friendly numbers.

Moderate Predictions

Pivoting away from rounding numbers, the next lesson is how to make moderate predictions and recommendations.

As a consultant, you should constantly strive to see both sides of an argument. Train yourself to poke holes in assumptions and question ideas. You should not only envision how a company will succeed, but also how it could fail. Extreme assumptions or recommendations (e.g., "it's my way or the highway") have no place in consulting. For this reason, you should strive for moderate predictions during the case interview.

MYTH: CONSULTANTS DON'T WORK ON FRIDAYS.

Most firms encourage practitioners to come into the consulting office on Fridays to network with peers. While Fridays are flexible and often more relaxed than the other workdays, clients need to know that their consultants are still available and productive!

Case Study: Wanderlust Inc.

Wanderlust Inc. is an online travel agency (OTA) based in Silicon Valley, California. Their revenues peaked in 2010 at $300 million and then steadily declined by about 6 percent each of the past 5 years. Despite this drop, Wanderlust has maintained its position as the fourth largest player in the OTA industry. This is because the industry overall has seen declining sales in varying degrees, with the larger companies experiencing a 2 to 4 percent decline annually, and smaller companies performing twice as poorly. In the current state, Wanderlust's board of directors is pressuring leadership to pursue one of two options: acquire or be acquired.

As a consultant for Wanderlust, your intuition should kick in immediately with a feeling of unease over the board's polar options. Acquire or be acquired? No other alternatives? As we've discussed in earlier chapters, there are many internal and external factors at play that could affect sales. Are Wanderlust's prices too high? Have prices changed? Are consumers moving away from OTAs in favor of going directly to airline or hotel websites? Have airlines and hotels changed their compensation

---

MY INTERVIEW STORY

"My consulting interview process was stressful, but making an effort to loosen up was a big help. I knew going in that my background, experience, and whether I was the right fit—along with my performance on the case interview—were all under scrutiny. During my interviews I had good, casual conversations with the interviewers and other interviewees, and this made all the difference. In the reception area, talking with other candidates put me at ease and made a good first impression with interviewers. Interviewers overlooked a few mistakes in the case because I had established rapport with them at the beginning of the interview. After all, being personable under stress is a requirement for the consulting profession."

Senior Consultant, Ernst & Young

or fee structure when partnering with OTAs? Have advertisers moved away from OTA websites?

The list of questions could go on and on. You would also need to understand potential acquisition targets and acquirers and further probe the core competencies, organizational structure, and financials of each. After probing into all three areas—Wanderlust, acquisition targets, and potential acquirers—you would then present a moderate prediction as an alternative to the board of directors. For example:

"After analyzing Wanderlust Inc., we found that your online website traffic is increasing while sales are decreasing. In other words, more people are visiting the site but fewer people are buying. This is due to an out-of-date technology platform, which encounters more technical difficulties than those used by competitors, thus driving customers away from the site before purchase. However, Wanderlust has strong brand equity and a world-class marketing team. Combining these two factors, I suggest that Wanderlust consider an alternative strategy: Migrate to a new online platform while retaining the current marketing strategy. This will enable the company to retain brand equity while providing a more positive customer experience to increase sales."

This example shows a moderate prediction between the two extremes of acquiring or being acquired. It uses analysis and creativity to come up with a recommendation that avoids polarization.

LEARNING TARGETS:

◎ *Use friendly numbers—round, even integers—to make the math as uncomplicated as possible.*

◎ *Practice math equations that employ percentages or fractions.*

◎ *Strive for moderation predictions.*

RECAP OF DAYS 20 THROUGH 11

Congratulations on completing the first half of your case interview preparation. We understand that you may be suffering from information overload
right now, but don't stress. This spread provides a quick synopsis of the
lessons, frameworks, and techniques you've learned to date. Think of this
as an interview-day cheat sheet.

Fundamentals

There are four basic components to nailing any case interview: listening,
communicating in baby steps, using full cognition, and applying funneled
thinking.

Listening is critical during the case interview. Employ your active listening
skills to ensure that you take down all of the critical information in the case
prompt, understand the questions being asked, and pick up cues on any
information your interviewer might be withholding.

Communicate through baby steps so that you don't get ahead of yourself
or your interviewer. By walking the interviewer step by step through your
reasoning, you take control of the interview's pace. Consequently, you will
solve the problem more effectively. Avoid logical jumps by always stating your
underlying assumptions.

Use full cognition to find creative and logical solutions. To employ the
combination, you must trust your intuition, verify through reasoning, and then
test your reasoning.

Apply funneled thinking to your responses. Brainstorm a variety of high-
level responses before homing in on one solution. Avoid the common case
interview mistake of identifying one cause for a problem without considering
alternatives.

Profitability Framework

The simple equation Revenue − Cost = Profit can be used to solve an array of
challenges. Ensure that you understand the key components that influence
each factor:

$$\text{Price} \times \text{Volume} = \text{Revenue}$$
$$\text{Variable Costs} + \text{Fixed Costs} = \text{Total Costs}$$

When analyzing revenue, consider price and volume. For price, compare
a company's prices related to its competitors' and inquire about any recent

price fluctuations. For volume, seek to understand not only how sales volume has fluctuated but also *why* it may have fluctuated.

When analyzing costs, consider both fixed and variable costs. Fixed costs, such as salaries, mortgages, and facility overhead, exist in the absence of sales. Variable costs increase as units produced increase and include raw materials, labor, and distribution costs.

Finally, when assessing profitability, you must take all factors into account. Use the profitability framework when you hear phrases like "declining margins," "rising costs," or "growth issues."

Internal/External Framework

Apply the internal/external framework to expand beyond a simple profitability issue.

When assessing internal challenges that a company may face, consider people, product, process, and technology. When assessing the external environment in which a company operates, look at customers, market, competitors, and risk.

During the case, you don't need to spend too much time assessing all eight factors listed above. Instead, use this framework in conjunction with funneled thinking to consider the internal and external factors at a high level and then as a way to identify the areas that seem most important to analyze further.

Rock Star Case Interview Techniques

Most recently, you learned several techniques for navigating the case. First, you learned to categorize and group your responses. Using the two key frameworks, we picked several focus areas and categorized them. Then we grouped our logical reasoning steps into those categories. You also learned that the truth lies in the middle. Instead of struggling with exact numbers or extreme recommendations, strive for rounded figures and moderate predictions.

Finally, by focusing on organizing your thoughts and remaining flexible while solving problems, you avoid boxing yourself into a specific framework. Remember, fit the framework to the case and not the case to the framework.

As you move into the home stretch of preparation, you will learn more techniques to polish your interview skills.

Keep up the great work!

~~20~~ ~~19~~ ~~18~~ ~~17~~ ~~16~~ ~~15~~

~~14~~ ~~13~~ ~~12~~ ~~11~~ ~~10~~ 9 8

7 6 5 4 3 2 1

10

DAYS

Mock Interview No. 5

Read through the following script with a friend or classmate. Next, review the instructions for live case practice on page 166. When ready, have your partner use the interview guide on page 172 to lead you through the case as if it were an actual interview.

Interviewer: *Longhorn Oil Corp. is an integrated, multinational energy company based in Texas that focuses solely on oil and natural gas. Longhorn Oil has substantial assets that make it a dominant player in its field, with annual revenue exceeding $200 billion and more than 60,000 employees. It operates in 47 countries and has corporate headquarters in Houston, Dubai, São Paulo, and Singapore. Longhorn Oil's size, however, prevents it from adjusting quickly to the innovative moves of its competitors. Recently, another major energy firm announced a new initiative to invest in renewable energy. The competitor plans to spend $5 billion over the next three years on wind and solar farms to diversify its energy holdings and generate goodwill with the public. Our client's leadership team is* *concerned that Longhorn Oil may miss out on the opportunities of tomorrow, and they have asked for our help to assess if they should enter the renewable energy market.*

Candidate: Do you mind if I take a moment to review the information I've captured?

Interviewer: *Go right ahead.*

Candidate: If it's okay with you, I'd like to repeat the background details to ensure I haven't forgotten or missed anything. Our client is Longhorn Oil Corp., a major global player in the energy business, specifically oil and gas. The company is massive, with more than $200 billion in revenue and 60,000 employees. The client's size gives it many resources, but inhibits its ability to react to market innovations.

Interviewer: *That sounds right to me.*

Candidate: Perfect. I do have a clarifying question. What do you mean when you say that Longhorn Oil is "integrated"?

Interviewer: *"Integrated" is short for vertically integrated, which means that the company fills multiple roles in the energy supply chain, as opposed to just one. For example, Longhorn Oil not only discovers and extracts natural resources, but also transports and refines those resources later in the supply chain. Can you take a guess at what it means to be horizontally integrated?*

Candidate: I imagine that a horizontally integrated company is one that dominates one step of the supply chain, almost like a monopoly.

Interview: *What's an example of such a company?*

Candidate: Perhaps a large media company that owns a variety of news outlets. With radio stations, television channels, magazines, blogs, and newspapers, such a company would have a major influence on the type of news people receive.

Interviewer: *Quite true. That example in particular demonstrates the danger of a monopoly. But we digress. Please, continue.*

Candidate: Right. Is it okay if I take a few minutes to determine my approach?

Interviewer: *Not a problem.*

Candidate: Okay, from our client's request, it seems that we need to capture more information about the renewable energy market. Since we're not diagnosing a profitability issue, I'm going to take a broader approach toward collecting information. Specifically, I'd like to learn more about the internal and external forces that will influence Longhorn Oil's incentive and ability to execute a renewable energy strategy. My internal focus will be on product and people. We need to learn more about the product's economics and what it takes to successfully enter such an innovative research space. Externally, we should seek to learn more about the energy market and risks. Analyzing market trends will allow us to compare the renewable opportunity to other options. At the same time, seeking to uncover potential risks will ensure that we don't make a possibly damaging recommendation to our client. If any of these avenues looks promising, we can dive deeper in that vein.

Interviewer: *That sounds like a reasonable approach to me.*

Candidate: Great. Starting with the product, what do we know about the economics of renewable energy? Is it profitable at this stage, or is the hope to further research and develop until the technology becomes efficient enough to produce scalable profits?

Interviewer: *Without subsidies, wind and solar power can't be produced profitably at this time. However, researchers estimate that within a decade, scientists will develop the technology necessary to efficiently capture and store renewable energy, making it competitive with oil or gas.*

Candidate: That tells me that our key competitor is making a long-term bet as opposed to seizing an existing opportunity. However, it seems unlikely to me that a company would invest so much capital without at least the prospect of a near-term financial benefit. I know recent political administrations have been pushing hard for companies to further develop renewables. Is there federal or state government funding available to companies investing in renewable energy?

Interviewer: *Through a federal government program, our competitor can write off taxes on all $5 billion spent on their project.*

Candidate: That certainly is an attractive incentive. Perfect. Now that I understand the "why," I'd like to shift focus to the "how." Does Longhorn Oil have any experience in the renewable space? Does the company have the human resources necessary to conduct additional research in this field and compete with our main competitor?

Interviewer: *Our client had an unsuccessful foray into thermal energy six years ago. Since then, management has focused purely on oil and natural gas. Concerning a research team, Longhorn Oil has no strong candidates within its ranks to execute the effort. Do you think this is a major hurdle for the company?*

Candidate: Well, yes, for two reasons. First, with no existing employees who have the necessary skill sets, our client will need to spend a year or two building and training a capable team. Second, Longhorn Oil will have to create an organizational and physical space that allows the team to function outside the boundaries of an oil company but still maintain oversight and sufficient resources. Such a move could result in negative responses from the existing oil- and gas-focused research teams employed by the company.

Interviewer: *Well said.*

Candidate: I believe I have a solid base understanding of the internal factors and challenges. Shifting our analysis to external factors, what trends has the overall energy market seen over the past three to five years, both in terms of financial performance and in general observation of the industry?

Interviewer: *What do you mean by "general observation of the industry"?*

Candidate: Apologies, I didn't mean to be vague. I'd like to learn if there have been any major market events such as mega-mergers, technological breakthroughs, game-changing discoveries, and catastrophic failures.

Interviewer: *Understood. Concerning financials, mergers, and failures, the industry has experienced nothing outside the norm of the standard oil and gas cyclicality experienced throughout the last several decades. Booms and busts, busts and booms. There have been some tech breakthroughs related to renewable energy, but as I mentioned earlier, none of these has resulted in a scalable, profit-able energy platform. There have been discoveries of new oil and gas fields, both offshore and through the hydraulic fracturing of shale, also known as "fracking."*

Candidate: Based on that information, would it be safe to say that Longhorn Oil is accustomed to navigating the current state of the energy industry?

Interviewer: *I would say so.*

Candidate: Interesting. To recap what we've learned thus far, Longhorn Oil's management is considering whether to invest in the renewable energy space. The main impetus of this question stems from a key com-petitor, who chose to leverage federal government tax benefits to make a $5 billion investment in the wind and solar power space, despite the unprofitable nature of current renewable technology. Longhorn Oil has no previous experience or in-house knowledge concerning renewable energy, and it isn't experiencing any industry pressures beyond the norm for major oil and gas companies. From what I've deduced at this point, it seems that our client's principle risk is that it may choose not to invest in technology that could displace oil and gas as the principle energy source in the coming decades.

Interviewer: *Thorough synopsis, but light on numbers. How can we quantify Longhorn Oil's two options? If the company fails to invest today, how might it successfully avoid missing the opportunity in the future?*

Candidate: I'm not sure I understand what you mean by two options. Invest or not invest?

Interviewer: *Let me try a different angle. What are two ways a company can acquire new capabilities?*

Candidate: Ah, I see. Either through organic development, such as building a new team, or through acquisition.

Interviewer: *Precisely.*

Candidate: Okay. I'd like to assume that Longhorn Oil would need to invest $5 billion, the same amount as its competitor, if it were to develop renewable capabilities in-house. Is that a safe assumption?

Interviewer: *Yes, I'm comfortable with that.*

Candidate: Great. With that, let's assess the acquisition prospects. I assume that Longhorn would look to acquire a smaller company that specializes in renewable energy, most likely a start-up. Do we have any figures that may help us to value a renewable energy start-up for acquisition?

Interviewer: *We do. There is a company based in San Diego, California that is considered the most innovative developer of wind and solar energy technology. We can use this company as a benchmark for a valuation. What type of data do you need to determine the value of an enterprise?*

Candidate: Honestly, I'm not terribly familiar with financial valuation. I imagine we would want to use the company's revenues, but I'm not sure how.

Interviewer: *That's fine. In finance, we use what are called "valuation multiples" to quickly estimate the value of an enterprise. Simply put, the multiple is a multiplier applied to a given company's revenue. Each industry has a different range of possible multiples based on future growth prospects and past performance. In this case, we want to apply a valuation multiple that's commonly used for American start-ups in the renewable energy space. Can you guess where we might find the number we need?*

Candidate: I imagine that investment companies are constantly valuing potential opportunities. Perhaps the investment companies publish reports that outline their opinions on a given firm or industry to drive more business?

Interviewer: *Good example. We know from analyst reports that in five years, the California-based company is expected to generate $84 million in annual sales. The standard valuation multiple used is 45 times revenue.*

Candidate: Okay, that means the company could likely be purchased for about $80 million multiplied by 40, or $32 billion.

Interviewer: *Can you double-check that calculation for me? Also, can you please stick with $84 million and a multiple of 45 rather than rounding? Take your time.*

Candidate: My mistake. First, I'll break down the number to make our calculations more manageable. So, $80 million multiplied by 40 is actually $3.2 billion. And $80 million multiplied by 5 is $400 million. Together, that's $3.6 billion. Then, $4 million dollars multiplied by 40 is $160 million, and $4 million dollars multiplied by 5 is $20 million. Together, that's $180 million. All together, we have $3.6 billion plus $180 million, which gives us a total company valuation of $3.78 billion.

Interviewer: *What percentage savings does that represent over the $5 billion investment option? Feel free to round this time for ease of calculation. Also, let's keep it simple and ignore the tax benefit.*

Candidate: The difference of roughly $1.2 billion divided by $5 billion represents just under 25 percent in savings.

Interviewer: *Based on what we know and your knowledge of acquisitions, what's your recommendation for Longhorn Oil?*

Candidate: Is it okay if I take a few minutes to gather my notes?

Interviewer: *No problem.*

Candidate: Great. We began our competitive response assessment by analyzing the profitability projections for the renewable energy industry, as well as considering the tax benefits granted to our client's key competitor. We also considered the time, expense, and organizational change required to build an in-house renewable energy research team, and we developed an estimate for what it would cost to acquire similar capabilities from a renewable energy start-up.

Given this, I recommend that Longhorn Oil wait until wind and solar power technology is more advanced, at which point our client should acquire a leading start-up in the industry. The advantage of doing so is to delay a major capital expenditure until the opportunity is better defined and save money through acquisition rather than organic development. This approach also allows Longhorn Oil to focus on its core business of oil and natural gas in the meantime.

Interviewer: *Excellent. Any potential pitfalls to your recommendation? We're running low on time, so just give me one.*

Candidate: One potential risk or pitfall of waiting to acquire a company is that its valuation may increase substantially once the technology is better defined. To mitigate such a risk, I would recommend that Longhorn Oil reassess the acquisition opportunities every three to six months and stay ahead of any major breakthroughs that may affect valuation.

Interviewer: *Excellent. Thank you. That concludes our case. Any questions for me in our last few minutes?*

Candidate: That was a fun case to solve. I'm quite interested in renewable energy. What opportunities exist at your firm to work in that industry?

Interviewer: *I don't work in that area, but I have a great friend in the Denver office who would be a good person for you to contact. Her name is . . .*

9

Show Your Leadership

Have you ever been in the same room with an executive? If so, what did you notice about that person?

Perhaps you saw confidence, charisma, and assuredness. Perhaps you noticed power, dominance, and a slight intimidation factor. Most successful professionals exude all of these qualities. But maybe you noticed something else, something less obvious but equally crucial: curiosity.

Two signs of a strong leader are a desire to learn and an ability to ask questions about the world. Leaders don't assume that they have all the answers. Instead, they surround themselves with intelligent people to bolster their deficiencies and challenge their skills. Leaders don't accept "facts" at face value; they ask questions and poke holes to understand the underlying assumptions and potential errors in an argument's logic.

Clients hire consultants for this type of leadership. You must demonstrate this capability during the case interview. One way to do so is to master the art of asking questions.

There is no such thing as the right question; there is only the right dialogue. Having the courage to ask questions can often be a challenge.

However, once you find that courage during the case interview, you'll uncover a treasure trove of useful information and, just as important, build rapport with your interviewer.

FAQs About Asking Questions

During the interview, it is more important for you to ask questions than to be afraid of asking a stupid one. Be thoughtful about the type and phrasing of the questions you ask. Slow down, take your time, and ask probing questions that facilitate a good exchange of ideas. This will also help you build a relationship with your interviewer. It will not only improve your chances at solving the case, but you'll also build an ally to support you when a decision on a final offer is made.

Q: When can I ask questions?

You can and should ask questions throughout the entire interview. In fact, don't wait until midway through to clarify information that you don't understand. Verify your understanding of the information right away. The earlier you ask questions, the more comfortable and confident you will feel with the case because questions allow you to master the content while controlling the interview's pace and tone.

At the beginning, ask *clarifying* questions:

- Can I confirm a few facts with you from the case prompt?
- You said that revenues declined over the past few years, but do we know by how much?

- You mentioned that our client is headquartered in Hong Kong. Does it operate in any other major geographies?

- I heard you say that our client dominates the industry for luxury female athletic gear. Can you clarify what "luxury" refers to in this context?

- You said that the client controls 40 percent of the marketplace for toys. Is that domestic or international?

After you grasp the information, ask *probing* questions:

- Do we know why the board of directors is pushing for change in such a compressed timeline? Are there any external factors at play?

- Our client's profit margins are slipping. Do you know if competitors are experiencing similar challenges?

- Our client clearly has an issue with wasting inventory that doesn't sell on a daily basis. Do we know if reducing inventory would put sales at risk?

- Sales volume seems to be challenging for our client. Have we seen any fluctuations throughout the year due to cyclicality or seasonality?

You should ask probing questions throughout the entire interview to engage your interviewer in an interesting dialogue and drive you to the root of the case.

Q: What questions should I ask myself internally about the case?
To remain on track, try to consider each of the following questions:

- What is the client's objective as a company?

- What facts do I have about the situation?

- What is the key problem the client is asking me to solve?

- Am I following my framework?

- What are obvious, conservative solutions?

- What are creative, bolder alternatives?

- What are the consequences of each potential recommendation?

- Which recommendation leads to the best possible outcome based on the client's objective?

A publicly-traded consulting firm with global size and scale, Accenture differentiates itself by operating at the intersection of business and technology. Having pioneered systems and business integration, Accenture offers a range of consulting services including strategy, digital, technology, and operations. The firm espouses a culture of innovation and hires thousands of PhDs, data scientists, Web developers, and digital marketers each year. These experts fill multiple research and development technology labs across the globe, investigating new technologies to predict the business solutions of tomorrow.

You can ask yourself the first three questions immediately after hearing the case prompt. The remaining questions should be your focus during the rest of the case.

Q: When should I ask for additional data?
Whenever you approach a quantitative question, ask your interviewer if she can share additional figures. Be specific.

- Do we have sales figures for any of the last three years?
- Do we know the total market size for leather coats?
- Has the client provided us with data on their inventory-wastage costs?

Even if your interviewer doesn't have the exact figure you request, she will point you in the right direction. Remember that if you're asked to estimate figures, pick friendly numbers in your assumptions to simplify the calculations.

Q: How can I phrase a question to get the most information from the interviewer?
Ask probing, open-ended questions that can't be answered with a simple "yes" or "no." The goal is to not only gather information, but also to encourage a dialogue. No interviewer wants to spend an hour listening

to a candidate drone on about pricing strategies. Examples of effective phrasing include:

- I'm not familiar with the term "leverage." What is an example of a highly leveraged company?
- How would you characterize our client's target market?
- How does the client's value proposition differ from its competitors'?
- Have you ever worked with a client who faced a similar challenge to the one presented in this case? How did you advise the client in that situation?

While you want to avoid unnecessary tangents, open-ended questions can provide you with more information about the case. Keep in mind that your interviewer has a plethora of experiences from which to pull, even if she doesn't work in the specific industry discussed in the case.

Q: Will I be able to ask questions not related to the case during the case interview?

If time permits, most interviewers are eager to answer non-case questions at the end of the interview. Firms don't want you to leave the interview with burning questions. If you run out of time, ask for

---

MY INTERVIEW STORY

"Learning how to do a case interview was both challenging and rewarding. Challenging, because I didn't think or communicate naturally in the systematic and structured manner expected by management consulting firms; rewarding, because I immediately recognized the value of such analytical and communication approaches outside of a case interview. I began to seek Mutually Exclusive and Collectively Exhaustive (MECE) structures in my papers and number my points in a class discussion in my senior year, and I believe my new habits were the reasons that my final year was my most academically successful year as an undergraduate."

Associate Consultant, The Bridgespan Group

Depending on the firm and economic environment, new-hire consultants can make $60,000 to $100,000 in salary, bonuses, and benefits during their first year. This pales in comparison to the hourly rates charged to clients that can range from $150 to $300 based on the size and nature of the engagement.

---

your interviewer's business card so that you can follow up via email. This is a best practice for another important reason as well: writing a thank-you note.

When you ask questions not related to the case, focus on topics you are genuinely interested in and that you can't research online. Your authenticity will show. The best questions will allow your interviewer to share personal anecdotes and insights that will be invaluable for you as a candidate. For example:

- What excites you about going to work every day?
- Where do you see growth opportunities in the consulting industry?
- Is there anything about your job that keeps you up at night?

Q: Is there really *no such thing as a stupid question?*
This statement is true, but with a small caveat: Don't ask your interviewer questions that you could have researched before your interview.

LEARNING TARGETS:

◎ *Ask clarifying questions in the beginning and probing questions throughout the interview to demonstrate your confidence and leadership.*

◎ *Stimulate dialogue with your interviewer by asking open-ended questions.*

◎ *If quantitative analysis is needed, query your interviewer for additional data that might be helpful.*

◎ *Inquire about the company and the profession at the end of the interview.*

CASE INTERVIEW IN

8

DAYS

Mock Interview No. 6

*Read through the following script with a friend or classmate.
Next, review the instructions for live case practice on page
166. When ready, have your partner use the interview guide
on page 174 to lead you through the case as if it were an
actual interview.*

Interviewer: **Telechatter Inc. is an American telecommunications
company based in Seattle, Washington that provides cellular communication services to 10 percent of the American population.
Operating a nationwide network of cellular towers, Telechatter competes with a handful of domestic competitors for contracts to relay
data to and from customers' devices. Despite their strong position,
over the past two years, Telechatter has experienced a decline in sales
that threatens to derail the company's five-year strategic plan. Our
team has been hired to determine what is causing the revenue decline
and suggest a potential solution.**

Candidate: May I take a few minutes to familiarize myself with the
information?

Interviewer: *Not a problem.*

Candidate: If you don't mind, I'd like to repeat the background details to ensure I haven't forgotten or missed anything. Our client is Telechatter, a telecom company that competes in a fairly consolidated market to provide wireless coverage through their cellular tower system. While Telechatter has 10 percent penetration of the market, recently the company has seen a decline in sales, and they've hired us to identify and solve the problem before it derails their five-year plan.

Interviewer: *Correct.*

Candidate: Perfect. Do you mind if I take a moment to consider my approach?

Interviewer: *Go ahead.*

Candidate: Based on what I've heard, I'd like to first focus on why revenue is declining. We'll do so by considering the two components that determine revenue: volume and price. Next, we'll conduct an internal/external analysis by zeroing in on the product, overall market, competitors, and customers. If one of these avenues seems to be the obvious pressure point, we'll dive more deeply into that area. How does that approach sound to you?

Interviewer: *I like it. Let's dive right in.*

Candidate: As I mentioned before, revenue is split into two components. Let's start with volume. Has Telechatter experienced any major declines in its customer base over the last three to five years?

Interviewer: *Telechatter's total cellular plans dropped by two million customers two years ago and 1 million customers last year. What percentage drop does this represent if the United States population using cell phones is 200 million?*

Candidate: If the client has captured 10 percent of a 200 million population...

Interviewer: *Is 10 percent the right number to be using?*

Candidate: Good point. Telechatter's market penetration is currently 10 percent, which takes into account the two years of declines. What was their previous market share? Can we assume the United States population using cell phones remained the same?

Interviewer: *About 12 percent, and yes, that's a fair assumption.*

Candidate: If the client previously captured roughly 12 percent of a population of 200 million people, then their total market size was 24 million customers 2 years ago. Subtracting the decline of 3 million customers, Telechatter is left with a total of 21 million customers. In terms of the company's customer base, a 3 million decline was equal to ... let's see, rate of change is equal to the change in volume over the initial volume, so 3 million divided by 24 million, which comes out to ... between a 12 and 13 percent drop over 2 years.

Interviewer: *Correct.*

Candidate: That's a major issue we'll want to learn more about. Perhaps it's being driven by prices. Have there been any changes to pricing over those two years?

Interviewer: *Individual plans cost $80 per year, family plans cost $100 per year, and business plans cost $150 per year. None of these prices have changed recently.*

Candidate: Interesting. Then let's consider the product portfolio to see if we can identify which products are negatively affecting sales performance. Have there been any substantial changes to the product offerings recently?

Interviewer: *All three plans have experienced a decline in sales. Moreover, none of the plans have been adjusted in terms of content within the last two years.*

Candidate: Interesting. That rules out another potential factor then. Shifting to external factors, have we seen any new market trends, such as new technologies or major mergers? Have Telechatter's competitors done anything different recently, such as dropping prices or releasing new products?

Interviewer: *The overall market has continued to grow, while the competitive landscape has remained relatively static. Reflecting on the nature of the telecom industry, what are some reasons that explain these trends?*

Candidate: Do you mind if I take 30 seconds to list a few ideas?

Interviewer: *No rush.*

Candidate: Okay. Considering the massive popularity of smart devices, growth in the wireless market makes perfect sense. A static competitive landscape implies that there's something inhibiting new developments or competitors. In other words, there's some type of barrier to entry. Thinking back to the initial data we received, we know that Telechatter manages a network of cellular towers. Perhaps it's the high capital cost related to these towers that keeps the market from becoming more dynamic.

Interviewer: *That's exactly right.*

Candidate: From our initial focus areas, only one additional category remains: customers. Who are the client's customers? I imagine they all want the same thing: fast, reliable, and cheap wireless coverage. Are they satisfied with Telechatter's ability to fulfill these needs?

Interviewer: *Telechatter's customers are 73 percent individuals and families and 27 percent organizations such as businesses and governments. The company's satisfaction rates have remained competitive across the nation except for the Mountain West region, which has seen a 41 percent decline.*

Candidate: Wow, not good. Can you please define the Mountain West region? I'm thinking of the Rocky Mountains but want to be sure.

Interviewer: *Let's stick with that definition. Essentially the area is composed of mountain towns from Montana to Colorado and one major city, Denver.*

Candidate: Got it. Right, so we know that industry prices have remained stagnant. I hypothesize that the drop must be related to product. I can think of two areas that we can analyze: speed/reliability and customer service. Does this sound reasonable to you?

Interviewer: *I think it's a viable hypothesis. Let's proceed.*

Candidate: Great. I'm going to isolate my two variables, starting with the customer service side. Do we know if that particular region has its own customer service team, and if so, what their performance has been recently?

Interviewer: *All regions share the same offshore customer service team.*

Candidate: So that option is out. Thinking back to the speed and reliability of cell coverage, there are several reasons that our client's satisfaction could have dropped. Do you mind if I take a minute to list my ideas?

Interviewer: *Go right ahead.*

Candidate: Okay. There are three potential causes of cell coverage dissatisfaction that I'd like to analyze: changes to the company's towers, entrance of competitors to a formerly monopolized local market, and physical barriers to cell signals such as new skyscrapers. Changes to the company's towers or new physical barriers could negatively affect Telechatter's ability to transmit signals and therefore cause its customers to seek alternative cellular service options. The entrance of competitors to the Mountain West market could have driven customers away from Telechatter, despite there being no new technology or attractive pricing.

INTERVIEW

Interviewer: *For the sake of time, let me stop you there and provide some more information that relates to your three focus areas. First, there has been no significant damage, hardware upgrades, or software changes related to the Mountain West towers. Second, our client has been the dominant player in the Mountain West region for nearly a decade, but two other service providers have been in the area for the same period of time. We don't have reliable competitor data by geography, but anecdotally, these less popular service providers seem to have experienced an uptick in sales over the past two years. Finally, the only notable physical development near the client's towers is a new military base 50 miles from Denver.*

Candidate: Perfect, this is helpful information in that it affirms the hypothesis that market share has been transferred from Telechatter to competitors. This implies the service-quality issue is specific to our client. Do you have additional information on the military base? Perhaps there is some type of interference occurring due to its presence.

Interviewer: *We're aware that cellular signals can be interrupted by certain radio frequencies. We also know that military bases are heavy users of such radio frequencies, and that the timing of the disruption aligns fairly closely with the establishment of the base.*

Candidate: Based on these facts, I think it's safe to assume that the military base is the cause of our problem. There must be a radio frequency interfering with Telechatter's cellular signals going between the Denver metro area and their tower. This would cause poor service and result in high customer turnover as Telechatter users fail to renew their service plans. Instead, these customers seek better service from our client's competitors, who likely have towers placed outside of the interference range.

Interviewer: *That seems logical to me. What options are available to our client?*

Candidate: Do you mind if I take a second to draft my thoughts?

Interviewer: *Not a problem.*

Candidate: Okay. We have three options, each of which has a unique set of pros and cons. Our first option is to work with the military base to reduce the radio frequency output or adjust its timing. This is the most cost-effective option but also the most difficult to achieve since the execution relies completely on an outside party. Our second option is to relocate the tower or build another tower so that the military base doesn't interfere with the transmissions to and from the Denver metro area. This requires high capital expenses, but it has the highest likelihood of success since Telechatter has the power to test various locations for interference and adjust tower placement accordingly. Our third option is to develop a new transmission frequency that won't be interrupted by the military base's radio activity. I'm not an expert in the field, but I imagine it would require research, development, software, and hardware changes to make such an adjustment possible. My guess is that the third option would also require a great deal of capital.

Interviewer: *Let's assume that the second option is the only realistic path forward. The cost of relocating the cellular tower is $15 million. Do you recommend that Telechatter move forward with the project? Assume that the entire customer volume drop is attributable to the greater Denver metro area and only 20 percent of customers would return if service returns to the previous standard. Also assume that plan types are split evenly across the customer population, and each product type earns a profit margin of 10 percent.*

Candidate: Is it okay if I take a few minutes to gather my notes?

Interviewer: *No problem.*

Candidate: Great. We began our revenue assessment by determining the market-penetration changes experienced by Telechatter. We then analyzed the industry, competitors, and customer data, eventually uncovering a customer-satisfaction anomaly in the Mountain West region. The decrease in satisfaction was related to poor cellular service, which we learned was related to a military base's radio transmissions near the Denver metro area. The total volume decline so far this year is three million customers.

To best assess the tower relocation cost of $15 million, we need to know the profits Telechatter will lose if the current situation continues. First, we'll use the prices provided earlier in the case of $80, $100, and $150. Since the plans are spread evenly, we can take the total of the plan prices, $330, and divide by 3, giving us an average price of $110 per customer.

If Telechatter were to not relocate the tower, the company would miss out on 3 million customers at the $110 average sales price, which equates to $330 million. Applying a 10 percent profit margin, Telechatter would forgo $33 million in annual profits. This figure is conservative, as it doesn't take into account the likelihood that more customers would leave if poor service continues.

If Telechatter does relocate the tower, the company will re-attract 20 percent of these annual profits, or $6.6 million.

Given this, it is my recommendation that Telechatter undertake the relocation project, which will yield a positive return on investment in less than three years.

Interviewer: *That sounds like good advice to me. Before we wrap up, what is one step the client could take to increase their customer return rate of 20 percent?*

Candidate: The client could conduct a promotion offering discounts to customers who sign up for a cellular plan in the metro Denver area during the next year.

Interviewer: *Great, that's the end of our case. Do you have any questions for me?*

Candidate: I love that the case's central challenge was something as arbitrary as geographic location. In consulting, how often do you find that business solutions can be driven from nonfinancial levers?

Interviewer: *It's actually more common than one would think. In fact, just the other month . . .*

7

Hypothesize

You've deconstructed the case prompt and clarified the facts, you've applied a framework to gather more information, and you've asked the right questions to further your understanding. In this chapter, we'll focus on how to develop a hypothesis, test that hypothesis, and drive toward a recommendation.

Case Study: Brew Dog Brewing

Say your client is Brew Dog Brewing, a beer manufacturing and distribution company based in Boise, Idaho. Brew Dog has a number of retail beer lines, ranging from affordable, reduced-calorie pilsners to specialty IPAs. They hired you to recommend a marketing strategy for their lowest-cost product, Brew Dog Lite, which has struggled to meet the company's revenue expectations.

After hearing the case prompt, you decide to employ an internal/external framework to assess Brew Dog's product, marketing efforts, customers, and competition. You ask your interviewer: What differentiates Brew Dog Lite from other low-calorie pilsners? How long has Brew

Dog sold Brew Dog Lite? What forms of marketing does Brew Dog currently use?

Further, you begin asking about the external environment. Who has Brew Dog marketed Brew Dog Lite to in the past? Who buys the product? Are customers satisfied with the product? Who are Brew Dog Lite's main competitors? How does Brew Dog Lite's price compare to that of its competitors?

Using your framework to gather information, you learn that Brew Dog Lite is losing market share to its competitors. Then you ask yourself, Why? Based on what you've learned, you rule out price and customer satisfaction as potential causes.

Develop a Hypothesis

What could be the potential cause of the loss in market share? To start, think of a few possibilities. For example:

1. Brew Dog is targeting the wrong demographic with marketing efforts.
2. Brew Dog is targeting the right demographic but using the wrong marketing mediums.
3. Brew Dog is targeting the right demographic and using the right marketing mediums, but they are not doing enough marketing to be effective.

Write down all of your hypotheses so you can refer back later, if needed. Next, pick the hypothesis that seems most probable. This is the idea that you will be pressure-testing for the remainder of the case.

Testing Your Hypothesis

You decide to pick the hypothesis that Brew Dog is targeting the wrong demographic with marketing efforts. To test the hypothesis, you must begin a new line of questioning that is specific to this topic to gather relevant quantitative and qualitative information.

Arthur D. Little, Inc., one of the first management consulting firms, was founded in 1886 with a specialization in technical research. Similarly, McKinsey & Company, founded in 1926, initially focused on applying accounting principles to management before switching to strategic advising after splitting into two separate companies in 1939.

To test the demographic fit for Brew Dog Lite, consider the following market-sizing exercise. Your interviewer tells you that the total market for light beer is $10 billion, and Brew Dog Lite currently has a 2 percent share ($200 million in annual revenue), which has been driven by marketing efforts targeting low-income beer drinkers between the ages of 30 and 40.

Your hypothesis assumes that Brew Dog Lite is targeting Demographic X today and should target Demographic Y going forward. For your hypothesis to be true, Demographic Y should be more willing to purchase Brew Dog Lite than Demographic X.

You decide to compare the company's current marketing demographic to beer drinkers between ages 21 and 25 who currently attend or graduated from college. After asking your interviewer if he has any information on said criteria, you learn the following:

Demographic:	Demographic Y
Age Range:	21–25
Level of Education:	College
Beer Drinkers (as a % of total population):	25% of 16 million college students/recent graduates
Population Size:	4 million

Once you've determined your demographic population's size, you must place a value on it. Estimate the annual beer spend per capita.

Demographic:	Demographic Y
Population Size:	4 million

Annual Spend on	$20 per week × 52 weeks
Lite Beer per Customer:	= $1,040
Market Size:	~$4 billion
Population Size:	4 million

Therefore, if Brew Dog Lite is able to capture just 10 percent of this demographic, or $400 million, they can greatly increase their current market share. With these estimates in hand, you launch into a consumer analysis, searching for a clue that might indicate the younger population is more interested in the product than the current target market. You soon learn that the consumer surveys hint at a growing affinity for craft beers by drinkers aged 30 to 40 years, while low-calorie offerings are seen as much more attractive to the college-age generation.

Based on both quantitative and qualitative testing of your hypothesis, you revealed that Brew Dog Lite could reap massive gains by directing marketing efforts toward a new demographic. Even without exploring other factors, such as marketing mediums, you've gained solid evidence to support a possible solution.

Although it wasn't necessary in this case, remember to refer back to your alternative hypotheses if your original one is disproven during

CONSULTING WISDOM

"Successful consultants display similar characteristics. Here are three attributes that new consultants should embody. First, go above and beyond what is expected. If you become aware of a problem, go beyond merely acknowledging it to proposing different solutions and volunteering to take the lead. Second, show your thought process. If you begin pro-posing solutions, detail the pros and cons of each option to allow people to follow. Transparency builds trust and credibility. Third, view setbacks as opportunities and maintain a positive outlook. A completely smooth project is rare, so embrace the opportunity to be a problem solver at every turn while maintaining a positive energy that can power your team."

Drew C., Senior Associate, Strategy&

testing. If there isn't sufficient time remaining in the interview to fully test your second hypothesis, be sure to provide your interviewer with an outline of what you would explore further given additional time.

Driving Toward a Recommendation

Ending with a recommendation is critical during the case interview. You may have performed a brilliant cross examination of your interviewer and a flawless analysis of the data, but your job is not complete without a clean summary of the facts and a clear path forward for the client.

First, summarize the case findings.

"Brew Dog Brewing is a diversified brewing company with both high-end and low-end beers. Currently, the company is losing market share to competitors on its low-end product, Brew Dog Lite, which is marketed toward a low-income demographic of adults between 30 and 40 years old."

Next, state your recommendation.

"After determining the market size for college-age beer drinkers, we learned that there exists a sizable sales opportunity. Coupled with consumer research indicating this population's high interest in low-calorie beers, I recommend that Brew Dog Lite shift its marketing strategy to target this younger demographic. Doing so has the potential to more

---

FIRM PROFILE: OLIVER WYMAN

Oliver Wyman is a global firm with more than half its offices outside North America. This structure is supported by the company's staffing approach, which places consultants on projects based on development need regardless of their home office. Unlike many firms, cross-pollination throughout international offices is the norm at Oliver Wyman. The firm is known for its annual reports on industry trends such as financial services, media, technology, and global risk. In 2007, Oliver Wyman merged with Mercer Management Consulting and Mercer Delta, forming its current structure and expanding its management consulting capabilities.

than double their current market share and keep them competitive in the marketplace."

Finally, share any considerations that you would explore further if you had more time.

"With more time, I would consider specific marketing techniques for this younger demographic, such as a social media strategy. As a next step, I recommend that Brew Dog Lite's marketing team research new mediums for marketing to a 21- to 25-year-old customer base and how they could partner with university programs to promote their brand."

Hypothesizing is a key component of the case interview. Throughout the case, you will constantly make hypotheses without consciously thinking about them. However, now that you know the process for applying a hypothesis-based approach to the case, do it consciously. Systematically determine a list of hypotheses, test one (or more), and drive to a recommendation.

LEARNING TARGETS:

◎ *Create a list of hypotheses that may be causing your client's problem, then pick the hypothesis that seems the most probable.*

◎ *Test your hypothesis both quantitatively and qualitatively.*

◎ *Refer back to your alternative hypotheses if your first one is invalidated.*

◎ *Summarize the case findings before stating your recommendation.*

◎ *Outline other considerations you would explore further if given additional time.*

CASE INTERVIEW IN

6

DAYS

Mock Interview No. 7

Read through the following script with a friend or classmate. Next, review the instructions for live case practice on page 166. When ready, have your partner use the interview guide on page 176 to lead you through the case as if it were an actual interview.

Interviewer: *Our client is a State Department of Corrections (DOC) consisting of 93 jail facilities and 22 prisons, housing 63,000 inmates. Due to recent budget cuts, DOC leadership has been asked to reduce prison expenditures by 10 percent in 1 year. With a current annual cost per inmate that is already 15 percent lower than the national average, the state prison system is struggling to identify additional opportunities for cost cutting. Our team has been asked to assist the DOC team in reducing its $2 billion budget by 10 percent while still maintaining adequate care and security for its prisoners.*

Candidate: Do you mind if I take a moment to review the background data?

Interviewer: *Go ahead.*

Candidate: I'm going to repeat what I heard to ensure I didn't miss anything. Our client, a State Department of Corrections, has asked for our help to reduce its $2 billion budget by 10 percent over the next year. The DOC system currently manages 93 jails, 22 prisons, and 63,000 inmates, at an annual cost per inmate that is 15 percent lower than the national average.

Interviewer: *Correct. Before we move further, can you please calculate the target average cost per inmate in one year?*

Candidate: Of course. First, we'll reduce the $2 billion budget by 10 percent, which leaves us with $1.8 billion. Dividing that number by a rounded number of 60,000 inmates gives us a targeted average cost per inmate of $3,000. That seems low.

Interviewer: *Close, you're off by a zero.*

Candidate: My apologies, the target cost is $30,000.

Interviewer: *Perfect. Continue.*

Candidate: Do you mind if I take a moment to consider my approach?

Interviewer: *Go ahead.*

Candidate: Okay. Anytime we're considering costs, we look at two categories: fixed costs and variable costs. For both groups, we'll want to know the largest prison expenses and their growth over time. Next, we'll look at the prison system overall to better understand leadership priorities and regulations. Given the safety and quality concerns noted earlier, such constraints may affect our ability to lower costs. We'll also want to consider what other state prison systems have done to reduce their budgets. Once this analysis is complete, we should be able to identify the best path forward for DOC. How does this approach sound to you?

Interviewer: *Good thinking to include government-related constraints in our analysis.*

Candidate: Excellent. Starting with costs, what are the big-ticket items in prison systems?

Interviewer: *Can you think of some that might be important?*

Candidate: In terms of fixed costs, I imagine expenses like wages and benefits are high to compensate employees for the risk involved in their profession. Security infrastructure upgrades such as cameras, towers, and fences may also be significant. For variable costs, I'm thinking of expenses associated with maintaining the inmate population, such as clothes, laundry, food, and healthcare.

Interviewer: *Those are most of the key items. Here's the exact budget breakdown: 50 percent is spent on security and security-personnel wages, 20 percent on medical, 15 percent on food, 5 percent on laundry, 5 percent on parole activities, and 5 percent on admin/other. None of these have grown or shrunk substantially over the past several years.*

Candidate: What exactly are "parole activities"?

Interviewer: *The cost of preparing for and conducting parole reviews.*

Candidate: The number of parole reviews must be contingent upon the number of inmates, so we will consider those to be a variable cost. So parole reviews combined with our other variable expenses of medical, food, and laundry, represent 45 percent of the budget. Our fixed expenses of security, wages, and admin/other represent the remaining 55 percent. To put those into context, let's learn more about DOC operations. Are security personnel government or private employees?

Interviewer: *Government. Why is this important?*

Candidate: My understanding is that it is more difficult to reduce headcount in public organizations, so it will be harder to cut costs related to personnel if none are privately employed. How are security upgrades managed? Does the system have an internal team, or is it outsourced?

Interviewer: *The DOC system has several teams it employs across the state to manage things like construction, maintenance, security tests, and camera installations for all of its facilities.*

Candidate: What is the DOC leadership's view of security-related expenses? This could be a highly sensitive topic considering the potential fallout that would arise from a security failure.

Interviewer: *That's exactly right. Leadership is not interested in cutting any security expenses at this time.*

Candidate: Fair enough. Of the variable expenses, medical is a particularly large item in the budget. What drives these costs, physician salaries or medicine expenses?

Interviewer: *Salaries are tightly regulated to ensure prisoners receive adequate healthcare. Similar to the security issue, the state's politicians are careful to mitigate the risk of bad press stemming from sick prisoners.*

Candidate: So that road is closed as well. Let's change gears and take a look at what other prison systems are doing to lower their expenditures. Do we have any information on the prisons that are considered "best in class"?

Interviewer: *Not exactly. We do know, however, that a neighboring state has one of the cheapest cost-per-inmate rates in the country at $15,000. This is due in large part to successful labor negotiations and outsourcing healthcare to private providers.*

Candidate: Labor negotiations require too much time to help our cause, but I'm interested to learn more about the option of outsourcing. If we're able to lower the DOC's variable medical costs, that may be all we need to reach our goal of a 10 percent reduction. Do we have any information on how outsourcing is managed for the neighboring state's prison system?

Interviewer: *That system contracts low-volume doctors from the rural areas surrounding most prison facilities. Such physicians have lower bill rates and are often asked to cover multiple facilities within a given radius by scheduling once-a-week visits. Do you think this would be an attractive option for the DOC?*

Candidate: It may be, though based on what we know about DOC leadership, if such a system results in less healthy prisoners, that would be a deal breaker. What are the neighboring system's mortality rates compared to those at the DOC?

Interviewer: *As of last year, 22 percent higher.*

Candidate: My guess is that 22 percent is too large an increase for our client's risk appetite. It seems that there is no feasible cost-cutting opportunity related to physicians either.

Interviewer: *It seems that way, though I do like the idea of outsourcing. You may be on to something.*

Candidate: Our problem is the prickly political issues.

Interviewer: *What do you mean?*

Candidate: It sounds like all employees are publicly employed, which means that headcount reduction will be difficult to achieve in our limited timeframe.

Interviewer: *We only confirmed that security professionals were civil servants. Government contractors at each facility run all laundry and food services.*

Candidate: My mistake, I had assumed we meant all personnel. The term "contractors" implies that these workers are managed but not employed by the facility. Is that correct?

Interviewer: *It is.*

Candidate: Interesting. Then I hypothesize that outsourcing certain labor could lead to cost savings for our client. Do we have any information on the client's current costs compared to privately outsourced cost estimates?

Interviewer: *It just so happens that we have some information on that topic. Based on market rates, it would cost $1.50 per meal to feed DOC inmates using an outsourcer. On average, laundry costs would be cut by $100,000 per facility annually. Both of these figures include reduced headcount.*

Candidate: We need to compare those numbers to the current costs. Let's start with cost per meal. Since 15 percent of the $2 billion total budget is for food, the DOC has a food budget of $300 million. Dividing that by our rounded number of 60,000 inmates, the prison spends about $5,000 per inmate annually on food. That number divided by 365 days equals a little less than $15 per day, assuming three meals a day results in a final cost per meal of $5.

Interviewer: *Is that accurate? You did a lot of rounding during your calculations.*

Candidate: Factoring in our rounding, the actual cost is somewhere between $4 and $5 per meal. Even if we're conservative and compare the low-end of the range to the outsourced option of $2 per meal, the DOC would see a 50 percent reduction in food costs, or $150 million.

Interviewer: *Excellent work. That's a sizeable drop, but we're still not quite to the $200 million goal.*

Candidate: Let's see if adding laundry savings gets us to the 10 percent cost savings target. There are 115 total facilities in the DOC system. When multiplied by the average outsourced savings of $100,000, we get $11.5 million in savings. Combining laundry and food service out-sourcing brings us $161.5 million in cost reductions, about 8 percent of the $2 billion statewide budget versus the 10 percent asked.

Interviewer: *So close. In the five minutes we have left, can you brain-storm a few more ideas for ways to reach our goal?*

Candidate: Definitely. Do you mind if I take a minute to list some ideas?

Interviewer: *By all means.*

Candidate: Right. I'll start with more traditional ideas and go from there. My first idea involves instituting work programs for prisoners on good behavior. By teaching inmates culinary or tailoring skills, the state can provide them with a better chance of integration upon release and also can bring down costs by not having to hire professionals. Another idea would be to analyze medicine purchase to maximize the use of more affordable generic brands and make purchases in bulk. Thinking more creatively, prisons could focus on generating revenue to cover costs, rather than cost cutting.

Interviewer: *Can you expand upon that idea?*

Candidate: Definitely. With a population that is forced to contend with a limited selection of food and entertainment, there is going to be a huge desire for something new. What if prisons operated stores or vending machines that sold higher quality products? Prisoners with good records could be allowed to receive funds or even gift baskets from their families, or apply their earnings from a prison job. Built into the price of each item would be a tax that goes straight to the facility to pay for the storefront and machine. Once those costs are covered, the facility is earning a profit and saving taxpayer dollars.

Interviewer: *I can see such a program incurring both controversial and beneficial effects, and I love the creativity. To close, can you pro-vide a brief recap of our work up to this point?*

Candidate: Of course, I'll take just a few seconds to gather my thoughts.

Interviewer: *No problem.*

Candidate: We began our cost-cutting assessment by learning about the key prison expenses, both fixed and variable. We then used the leadership's priorities of safety and quality to narrow our focus to a few key buckets. After learning that a neighboring prison system has cut costs through outsourcing, we hypothesized that a similar route focused on food and laundry services could lower costs. After testing, we determined that we could lower costs by about 8 percent. To reach the remaining 2 percent, we brainstormed a variety of ideas that we could explore if given more time. In light of this, I recommend that the State Department of Corrections pursue outsourcing food and laundry services at a minimum and further consider our additional options once analysis is complete.

Interviewer: *Sounds reasonable to me. That's the end of the case. Before you step out, do you have any questions for me?*

Candidate: I was pleasantly surprised to see a government-related case, as I'm highly interested in public-focused initiatives. Can you tell me about your firm's government-consulting practice?

Interviewer: *Of course. In fact, a good friend of mine is director of our firm's federal practice, headquartered in Washington, D.C. . . .*

20 ~~19~~ ~~18~~ ~~17~~ ~~16~~ ~~15~~
~~14~~ ~~13~~ ~~12~~ ~~11~~ ~~10~~ ~~9~~ ~~8~~
~~7~~ ~~6~~ ~~5~~ 4 3 2 1

5

Build Your Case

Over the past two weeks, you've learned a number of frameworks and techniques for organizing your thoughts and solving the case. If you've felt confused, it's because some best practices run counterintuitive to instinct, and some lessons add layers of complexity that make it difficult to remember all the simple tricks we provided early on. In today's lesson, let's connect the dots by providing a simple structure for approaching each business case, using the techniques and frameworks you've already learned. You've likely followed a similar structure unconsciously when answering previous cases. The goal here is to highlight and formalize that path.

Below are the seven steps to solving a case.

1. Unwind the case prompt.
2. Develop a framework.
3. Collect data.
4. Form a hypothesis.
5. Test your hypothesis.
6. Summarize the case.
7. Make a final recommendation.

Founded in 1983 by three Bain & Company alums, L.E.K. is a boutique strategy firm based in London. As the only major consulting firm that has grown from a base in the United Kingdom, L.E.K. competes with European consulting powers such as Roland Berger as well as American firms worldwide. With fewer than 2,000 employees, the firm remains competitive through an intense focus on four major service offerings: strategy, mergers and acquisitions, operations development, and marketing consulting. A leader in consulting services targeting green initiatives, L.E.K. itself became the first major consulting firm to become carbon neutral in 2008.

Unwind the Case Prompt

The first step goes back to the first lesson you learned: Listen with intent. Write down all the facts of the case. Write out the key challenges and the main question. Ask your interviewer clarifying questions to ensure that you understand all the details.

Next, jot down your gut reaction, or intuition, to the prompt. Begin to reason through the challenges. Always ask yourself this one simple question: What is the problem I've been asked to solve?

Develop a Framework

After you understand the details, shift your focus toward developing a framework. The two frameworks on which this book focuses are the profitability framework and the internal/external framework. While there are many other frameworks to choose from, these two provide the flexibility to navigate the vast majority of cases you might face on interview day.

Your goal should be to fit the framework to the case, not the case to the framework. Using the themes we discussed around profitability and internal/external environments, pick a few central focus areas to explore. Categorize them into groups of logical reasoning and use that as your custom framework for the case.

Remember that your case may span both the profitability framework and the internal/external framework. In this scenario, categorizing and grouping becomes particularly important so that you stay organized while exploring multiple avenues of analysis.

Collect Data

After selecting a framework, use it to collect more data. You received limited facts during the case prompt, so your job is to investigate. In this step, you should focus on asking the right questions to probe for more information.

During data collection, you may or may not perform quantitative analysis. Let the interviewer's responses to your probing questions guide you in determining whether or not quantitative analysis is necessary. Don't worry. You'll get your chance to crunch numbers as the case progresses.

Additionally, you may have to adjust your framework as you learn new information. For example, let's assume your initial framework focused on internal product challenges and external competitor threats, but during data collection you realize that there may be some underlying regulatory risks that need further examination. Pivot your line of reasoning and begin probing into the regulatory environment. Don't be married to your framework.

FACTOID

The "airport test" is another means by which consulting recruiters analyze candidates. The test is a behavioral interview rooted in a hypothetical scenario common to consultants: Would the recruiter want to be stranded in an airport with the candidate? Small talk while networking will ensure you pass this assessment.

Form a Hypothesis

Once you've gathered sufficient information, think back on what you learned from the first step, "unwind the case prompt." What is the problem that you've been asked to solve?

Referring to this question, write down a few potential hypotheses on what the root cause of the central challenge might be. While you can have multiple hypotheses, each hypothesis should only have one variable. We call this "isolating the variable." This will simplify testing tremendously.

After writing down a few potential hypotheses, pick one to test first. Your pick should be based on one of two criteria:

- what seems most plausible
- what seems easiest to rule out

Sometimes the best approach is to quickly rule out one hypothesis to shift probability to another. However, don't waste your time testing a hypothesis that you know won't solve the case.

MY INTERVIEW STORY

"I first interviewed at McKinsey & Company two years before graduating college, and I received a 'see you later' because I lacked experience. A 'see you later' is neither an offer nor a rejection; it means that you have the potential to become a McKinsey & Company consultant, but that you are not ready. To gain experience, I studied abroad in Melbourne, Australia, and I did an internship in Barcelona, Spain, before successfully re-interviewing at McKinsey & Company one year later. When McKinsey & Company says 'see you later,' they really want to see you again. Listen carefully to the feedback you receive and act on it!

Robin L., Associate, McKinsey & Company

Test Your Hypothesis

Testing your hypothesis requires more than guessing, intuition, or even logical reasoning; it will likely involve quantitative analysis.

Some examples of ways to test your hypothesis include market sizing (as demonstrated in "Case Interview in 7 Days: Hypothesize" chapter), profitability analysis, price-sensitivity analysis, and "make" versus "buy" analysis. Testing your hypothesis should allow you to assign value to various outcomes so that you can prove or disprove your hypothesis.

If your first hypothesis proves to be incorrect, refer back to your list of hypotheses. Pick a different one to test. The key is to waste as little time as possible disproving one hypothesis before moving to another. Test your hypotheses only until you find a solution that sufficiently addresses the central challenge of the case.

Summarize the Case

Once you've determined your hypothesis, tested it, and focused on a potential solution, take a step back. Give yourself a few moments to review the facts you've gathered, from the case prompt all the way to your analysis.

Before you jump into sharing your brilliant findings and recommendation, verbally summarize the case. Recall the fundamental skills that will help with your summary: funneled thinking and baby steps. Recite the company background, key facts, and central challenge of the case. Then review your funneled thinking step by step so that your interviewer recalls how you started from a high level and then narrowed in on specific solutions.

Summarizing the case allows you to show the interviewer that you're comfortable synthesizing ambiguous data and communicating key takeaways. It ensures that everyone is on the same page. Such skills are critical to consulting. While this step may seem trivial in comparison to others, it's actually one of the most important moments of the interview. Use these fleeting minutes at the end of your interview to take a deep breath and build your confidence going into the final recommendation.

PROFILE OF A SUCCESSFUL CANDIDATE

Lydia Arias applied to several top-tier consulting firms while she was a senior at Princeton University, where she studied Spanish and Portuguese litera-ture. She was also a standout student athlete, maintaining a 3.75 GPA while competing on the varsity track and field team as a pole vaulter. During her undergraduate studies, she gained professional experience as a social media marketing intern at BlueWave Computing and as a learning consultant at the Princeton University Learning Center. In this interview, you'll discover what really made Lydia successful on interview day and during her three-year career at a top strategy consulting firm.

Q: We'd like to start with a question about your background. How did your experiences at Princeton affect your decision to pursue consulting?

What led me to consider consulting was a search for something that was missing in my academic life. I loved my studies in the Spanish and Portu-guese literature department and considered applying to PhD programs, but ultimately I held back because of a nagging sense of wanting to make an impact outside academia. I found a junior summer internship in marketing to test a realm of business that seemed to fit my creative side. Marketing wasn't my passion, but the internship did lead me down the right path. I took on the task of creating a business plan for the emerging social media marketing division of the company. The combination of strategic thinking and a tangible end goal was so engaging that I began to look into a field that I had heard students and recent alumni talk about: consulting. The more I learned about consulting, the more it felt like a fit. What ultimately sold me on the idea was comparing it to my work as a learning consultant at the Learning Center on campus. The job entailed one-on-one discussions with undergrads to discuss everything from time management to cognitive theory to tactics for working through problems or internalizing concepts. It was challenging and incredibly rewarding, and I could see the parallel to consulting.

Q: It sounds like each experience taught you something about yourself that led you to con-sulting. Once you decided to pursue this path, how did you prepare for the case interview?

I focused on live repetition, not only of cases, but also thinking through responses for possible interview questions and brushing up on math. When it came to case prep, I resisted the urge to simply read case examples and instead committed to regular, live practice. I reached out to alumni working in consulting for some high-pressure practice, but more often I ran through cases with classmates who were also interviewing for consulting.

Q: Would you advise candidates to put themselves in similar high-pressure situations?

Yes, absolutely. It's the best way to simulate interview day. Case interviews require thinking on your feet and problem solving under pressure. Doing well in that out-loud, high-ambiguity format is all about having done it so many times that the feeling no longer throws you off.

Q: We agree. Can you tell us about your experience on interview day?

I booked an early time slot for my interview. I thought about what I wanted the interviewer to know about me by the end of the interview. I thought about my reasons for pursuing consulting and the anecdotes that would show my work ethic, intellectual curiosity, and drive to be a great teammate.

As the first case began, I shrugged off my nerves by focusing on the excitement of working through a new problem. I didn't need to rely on any memorized framework and could think of the case as an opportunity to have an interesting conversation and show the interviewer what I would be like as teammate.

I explained that my choice of major came out of a drive to challenge myself, and I described all the skills I had gained that would apply well in consulting: creative thinking, communication skills, and the ability to gain "expert status" on a new topic quickly when bombarded with information.

I thanked the interviewer and chatted with him about his experiences on my way back to the lobby. I greeted the receptionist and had a warm conversation with another candidate as I waited for my second interview. I remember thinking that the friendly atmosphere in the office felt right and that I would enjoy working with the down-to-earth people I had met. For me, the interview process helped me get a better sense of the cultural differences between firms.

The second interview brought a more challenging case. I felt stumped a few times, but I didn't let it throw me off, and I asked questions to feel out the right direction. I walked out feeling good about the interviews.

I promised myself I wouldn't worry about whether or not I would get an offer, so I spent the weekend visiting a friend. Two days later, I got the call from my second interviewer.

Q: From your perspective, what have been the most rewarding and the most challenging aspects of being a consultant?

It's hard to separate the rewarding from the challenging. There's nothing like cracking a problem you thought was impossible or giving a compelling presentation when deep down you're all nerves. When I think about what has been challenging, I think about this idea of never getting comfortable. The work moves quickly, and expectations of what you'll be able to accomplish change every six months. I have also made lifelong friendships at my firm and found amazing mentors who have invested unbelievable time and energy in helping me succeed. I am incredibly grateful for those relationships.

Q: If you could pinpoint three reasons that you were successful, what would they be?

First, strong preparation. I was able to calm my nerves and let my personality come across on interview day because I had done so many practices cases and knew what it felt like to think on my feet while keeping it conversational.

Second, perseverance. When the case got complex, I kept a good attitude. This helped me come across as cool under pressure and allowed me to push through to ideas and solutions.

Third, confidence. I aimed to appear confident even when I was nervous. I stood up tall, which made me feel more confident.

I know you asked for three, but I want to give one more: enthusiasm. I think this is more important than most candidates realize. The interviewer wants to know that you really want to be there and that, when it comes to tough cases, you will be an asset rather than a detriment to team morale.

Make a Final Recommendation

Once you've eloquently summarized the case, end by sharing your final recommendation. Manage your time so that you leave about five minutes at the end of the interview for a case summary and final recommendation. Never leave without some sort of resolution.

Give your recommendation with conviction. Be confident that your reasoning and analysis is correct, and use evidence to back it up. As with the rest of the interview, be sure to communicate the recommendation clearly and concisely.

Finally, share any considerations that you would explore further if time permitted. This shows that while you feel you've given the client a solid recommendation and path forward, you recognize alternative solutions and open questions.

Going into your final mock case interviews, make sure that you're incorporating each component of the seven-step structure. And if time permits, review the preceding mock case interviews and see if you can apply the seven-step structure. You may find the case much easier today than you did the first time around.

LEARNING TARGETS:

◎ *Utilize the seven-step structure when approaching each business case: 1) Unwind the case prompt; 2) Develop a framework; 3) Collect data; 4) Form a hypothesis; 5) Test your hypothesis; 6) Summarize the case; and 7) Make a final recommendation.*

◎ *Give your recommendation with conviction and confidence in your analysis.*

CASE INTERVIEW IN

4

DAYS

Mock Interview No. 8

Read through the following script with a friend or classmate. Next, review the instructions for live case practice on page 166. When ready, have your partner use the interview guide on page 178 to lead you through the case as if it were an actual interview.

Interviewer: *Our client, McSweet's Eats, is one of the largest cookie-baking companies in the United States. They make popular gourmet cookie arrangements. The company recently won a major sports contract that allows it to operate within a broad network of college and professional football stadiums over the next 2 years and retain 60 percent of the profits it generates. Based on McSweet's Eats' profitability during this trial period, the football stadium network may extend their contract by 10 years. If McSweet's Eats isn't able to contribute an average of $20,000 in profits to each stadium in the network, the contract will expire and a different vendor will take their place. The company's management team is confident that they can produce and distribute enough product to fulfill their contract, but* *they are nervous that football fans might be difficult to win over when there are more traditional food options available. Our team has been hired to develop a marketing strategy to maximize sales throughout the trial period.*

Candidate: Do you mind if I take a few seconds to organize my notes?

Interviewer: *Sure, take your time.*

Candidate: Okay, I understand that our client is McSweet's Eats, a major producer of cookie arrangements. Having recently won a trial two-year contract to sell their cookies in college and professional football stadiums, the company has hired our team to ensure they reach sales targets and earn a contract extension. Specifically, they would like for us to create a marketing strategy. Is that correct?

Interviewer: *That's it.*

Candidate: Great. I have one clarifying question: Are cookie arrangements the bouquets of cookies people send on special occasions like Valentine's Day?

Interviewer: *Correct.*

Candidate: Got it. May I take a minute to collect my thoughts and jot down some notes?

Interviewer: *Of course.*

Candidate: Considering our focus on marketing strategy, I'd like to target four specific areas for analysis within an internal/external framework. For internal, we'll analyze the product and pricing. Product refers to the cookie arrangements that McSweet's Eats sells, which may need to be altered from their retail versions based on cost of ingredients and size. By optimizing prices, we'll ensure our product can compete with other stadium food choices, yet still generate enough profits to satisfy McSweet's Eats and football stadium management. Externally, we'll look at positioning and advertising. Positioning is all about the physical location where the product is sold. In this instance, the decision is whether to sell via vendors or through storefront locations within the stadiums. Finally, advertising consists of the avenues used to capture customers' attention. Once we have a better understanding of these four areas, we'll be in position to identify the best route forward. How does that sound?

Interviewer: *Very thorough. Hopefully we have enough time to work through it all.*

Candidate: Good point. I'll keep my eye on the clock. Let's jump right in, starting with product. What's included in a retail cookie arrangement? Are there various offerings, such as basic and premium packages?

Interviewer: *Included is a set of a dozen cookies on stems, plastic-wrapped together and set in a small box that serves as a base. The most basic offering consists of one type of cookie, either sugar or chocolate chip, while the premium selection includes 12 unique gourmet cookies.*

Candidate: From that information, it sounds like there are several levers we could pull to drop cost for stadium-oriented arrangements. Do we have an itemized cost for the basic arrangement?

Interviewer: *It costs $0.50 per cookie, $2 for the base, $1 for the plastic wrap, and $0.10 per stem.*

Candidate: That leaves us with a total cost per cookie arrangement of $10.20. Moving on to pricing, what are the average prices of competing products in stadiums? I don't think hot dogs or burgers are as relevant as dessert items like hot chocolate, cotton candy, ice cream bars, and snow cones.

Interviewer: *We only have information on cotton candy and ice cream bars, which sell for an average price of $8 and $7, respectively.*

Candidate: Which means McSweet's Eats will have to lower product costs so that pricing can remain competitive. This could be accomplished in two ways. First, McSweet's Eats should eliminate the base, which is unnecessary in a ballpark environment where consumers have no surface on which to set the product. Second, the company should reduce the number of cookies, as these will be eaten over the course of a three-hour game.

Interviewer: *What would the new price look like after those changes?*

Candidate: Starting with $10.20, we subtract $2 for the base, leaving us with $8.20. Eliminating 6 cookies at $0.50 per cookie results in a further drop of $3, for a total of $5.20.

Interviewer: *And the stems?*

Candidate: Ah, thanks, I forgot about those. Reducing by 6 stems gives us another $0.60 in savings, for a final cost of $4.60 for a stadium arrangement. At that level, pricing won't be an issue.

Interviewer: *Agreed.*

Candidate: What about positioning? Where is McSweet's Eats allowed to sell the product within the stadium?

Interviewer: *The contract only allows for walking vendors, the number of which is set by each stadium.*

Candidate: Okay, it sounds like we don't have much flexibility there. Now we arrive to the core of the project: advertising.

Interviewer: *Before you continue, can you tell me about the standard promotional stunts used at stadiums?*

Candidate: Do you mind if I take 30 seconds to list a few ideas?

Interviewer: *Not a problem.*

Candidate: Great. I'll segment the promotional activities into two categories, passive or active. On the passive side, we have billboards, banners, cardboard cutouts, and advertisements via loudspeaker and video. Such advertising requires no action on the part of the fan and serves only as notifications that call attention to the product. Active promotion, on the other hand, requires more interaction with the fans. I'm thinking of shirt cannons, promo codes via text, interactive apps, and promoters handing out samples or ads. These are the types of advertisements that get people to physically act and therefore pay more attention to the product being sold.

Interviewer: *That's a thorough list. Which options should McSweet's Eats consider?*

Candidate: I hypothesize that McSweet's Eats should leverage a mixed strategy, employing both passive and active tactics. Given the prevalence of social media, McSweet's Eats could execute a mobile-based advertising campaign. For example, when fans comment in social media that they're at a game, advertisements could pop up for cookie bouquets. The physical action of commenting on social media will be an effective method for drawing attention to the product. Combining this promotion with more passive loudspeaker and video announcements will ensure the majority of fans are aware that arrangements are for sale. Through this strategy, and by keeping the price competitive by dropping product cost as we outlined earlier, I'm confident McSweet's Eats will be able to generate sufficient sales and earn a contract extension.

Interviewer: *I'm not so sure. Do you think that social media advertising will convince fans to buy McSweet's Eats products? Based on my own experiences, the market is saturated with this type of advertising, which means our clients won't be thrilled if we recommend something they likely have already considered.*

Candidate: I see. I guess I had a little social media tunnel vision there. Regarding advertising, we need something fresh.

Interviewer: *I think you're right to focus on active promotions where the fans are more involved. And that's not to say you can't somehow incorporate technology.*

Candidate: I agree. I like the idea of leveraging customers' smart devices. Even at games, people are glued to their phones. The problem is that no one would want to interact with their food vendor. What we need is something where fans are interacting with one another through McSweet's Eats.

Interviewer: *Go on...*

Candidate: Let's think about the cookie arrangement. Essentially, it mimics a flower bouquet. What if fans could send bouquets to each other? For instance, let's say I see an attractive individual a few rows ahead of me. What if I could send that person a bouquet via the vendor? Maybe I could even receive a discount or free cookie for doing so.

Interviewer: *Neat idea. I love that it connects people through the use of the product. But the market size is fairly limited in the scenario you just described. How could you increase the market to include the entire stadium and not just the people within eyesight?*

Candidate: McSweet's Eats could make an app similar to those used for dating. Anyone with the app will appear, and users could select people they "like." When two users match up, the pair could split a cookie bouquet at a discount. It could also allow users to share their seat number or message each other via a McSweet's Eats app. We'd be adding value to the product and empowering the customer to drive sales.

Interviewer: *Brilliant. It helps that the customer will be familiar with the process since similar applications already exist. Speaking of customers, can you estimate the amount of profits that your proposed app might produce per stadium per year? Assume that the price charged is the average of the two dessert products already sold.*

Candidate: Sure. I'll take a top-down approach, starting with the average stadium attendance. Based on my prior knowledge, I would say that on average about 80,000 fans attend a given college or professional football game. Of that total, I assume that about 10 percent of fans are under 18 years old, 30 percent are over 35 years old, and the remaining 60 percent are in-between. That leaves us with 48,000 fans that are in the prime dating age range of 18 to 35. We'll exclude fans already in relationships, as you wouldn't use the app to buy a bouquet for your partner sitting next to you. If the single population is 50 percent, then our total market population per game is 24,000 fans.

The average price of currently sold desserts is $7.50. Subtracting out the estimated cost per arrangement of $4.60 results in a profit of $2.90 per cookie arrangement sold. That profit, multiplied by 24,000 fans is . . . well, $2 multiplied by 24,000 is $48,000, and $0.90 multiplied by 24,000 is $21,600. In sum, the total market size in terms of profits is $69,600 per game. Assuming that there is an average of 10 games per regular season per stadium, McSweet's Eats can expect to earn $696,000 in profits per stadium each year. The stadium's cut is 40 percent, about $280,000.

Interviewer: *Is that the expected profit or the maximum profit?*

Candidate: My apologies, I misspoke there. Based on the filters we applied, the $280,000 represents the maximum profit opportunity. It's more realistic to assume McSweet's Eats might capture 10 to 20 percent of the maximum, assuming that our target group of single young fans may prefer different food options. So, McSweet's Eats can reasonably expect to generate around $28,000 to $56,000 in profit per stadium each year.

Interviewer: *Right. What is a potential risk of implementing this plan?*

Candidate: I always have cell service issues when attending large events. For this plan to work, consumers would need to have access to stadium-wide Wi-Fi, which would be too expensive to install for this use alone. The implication is that such an advertising strategy might work in only the stadiums equipped with Wi-Fi.

Interviewer: *Good point. Based on what we've learned, what is your recommendation to McSweet's Eats?*

Candidate: Is it all right if I take a minute to organize my thoughts?

Interviewer: *Not a problem.*

Candidate: Great. As you can see with the diagram I've sketched, we began developing a marketing strategy by analyzing the retail product so that we could better understand what we might adjust to make a stadium-tailored cookie arrangement. Next, we looked at pricing for competing products and identified a plan to lower the cost per arrangement sold. Then, we focused on advertising, considering both passive and active forms of attracting consumers' attention. From there, we had the idea to create a social media app that connects fans by allowing them to send and receive bouquets. Producing an estimated $28,000 to $56,000 in profits per stadium per year, this strategy represents an excellent opportunity for McSweet's Eats to receive a contract extension and exceed the target profit contribution of $20,000 per stadium.

Interviewer: *Perfect. That's the conclusion of our case. Before you leave, are there any questions I might be able to answer for you regarding our firm?*

Candidate: That had to be the most fun I've ever had on a case. What a neat client and challenge. Would you say the majority of your actual engagements are that interesting?

Interviewer: *I'll be honest, not all of them. But many are fantastic, and nearly all have an exciting component that provides an excellent learning opportunity and tests my . . .*

3

Make Your Point

If we were to assign points to various aspects of the case interview, the final recommendation would be worth a small amount. Assuming you've "shown your work" throughout the process (e.g., stated your assumptions, walked your interviewer step by step through your logic, and engaged in a healthy dialogue), the "correctness" of your final answer is less important. You've already earned close to full credit. That said, it is *absolutely critical* that you give a recommendation. Here's why.

Consulting is the business of helping leaders solve their most challenging problems. Yes, part of solving problems is identifying them. But in the end, clients pay large sums of money to get answers. During the case interview, you should give your recommendation with three main objectives in mind:

1. Demonstrate your ability to make evidence-based decisions.
2. Create a sense of resolution and finality to the case.
3. Emulate what you would do as a real-life consultant.

Until the end of the case, every piece of information you gather is evidence that you can use to draw a conclusion. Evidence is what supports your reasoning and either proves or disproves your hypothesis. Great consultants, and leaders in general, always use evidence to make decisions.

Case Study: Maple Leaf

Maple Leaf is a Canadian bank, headquartered in British Columbia. Twelve months ago, Maple Leaf's leadership signed a deal to acquire a midsize regional competitor, Big Bucks Bank.

Since agreeing to acquire Big Bucks Bank 12 months ago, Maple Leaf's leadership has created a large, transformational program office to manage integration planning. The program consists of three teams: product operations, human resources (HR), and technology. "Day One," or the day on which two companies become an official combined entity, is scheduled six months from today. However, leadership has a "go/no-go" decision one week prior to Day One. They hired your consulting firm to oversee the program office and help guide them to a "go/no-go" decision.

As a consultant, how should you advise such a critical decision with millions of dollars at stake? Should you make a subjective decision based on a gut feeling? Of course not. You should use evidence.

FIRM PROFILE: THE BRIDGESPAN GROUP

Created in 1999 by a former Bain & Company Managing Director and a Harvard professor, The Bridgespan Group is a nonprofit consulting firm that serves the nonprofit sector and philanthropists. With the goal of solving some of the toughest problems facing society today, The Bridgespan Group advises organizations in education, youth services, public health, philanthropy, and global development. Initially supported by grants from Bain & Company, the Bill & Melinda Gates Foundation, and other philanthropic foundations, the firm maintains a small team of roughly 200 consultants. However, Bain & Company consultants are permitted to spend 6 to 12 months interning with The Bridgespan Group through a special program.

WHAT NO INTERVIEWER WANTS YOU TO KNOW

By the time your interview rolls around, you likely will have prepared for nearly a month. Spoiler alert: your interviewer will not have done the same. Often, you both will be hearing the case for the first time that day.

Put yourself in the shoes of a busy consultant. It's Thursday at noon, and you're frantically finishing last-minute tasks and debriefing with your client before an afternoon flight. After a mad dash to the airport in rush-hour traffic, your flight is delayed. As the plane finally hurtles down the runway, you crack open the cases you'll be administering to candidates tomorrow. It's been a long week, and you accidentally fall asleep on the flight, missing your narrow window of opportunity to review the cases before tomorrow. The next morning, you scan the case during breakfast to get a base understanding of the problem. While you haven't memorized the numbers, you feel more or less ready. After all, you've administered hundreds of cases over your career.

This is the scene that unfolds before nearly every case interview. The reality is that interviewers are busy professionals trying to make deadlines and serve their clients' needs, which sometimes pushes interview preparation lower on their priority list. As a candidate, you probably won't notice that your interviewer is unfamiliar with the case. However, you may notice a pause or confused look that you mistake for a judgment on your performance. As often as not, these moments arise from the interviewer's own struggle as they learn the case on the fly while fielding your questions.

Despite your interviewer's ability to hide this weakness, use it to your own advantage in two key ways. First, take your time, whether it's for calculations

Demonstrate Your Ability to Make Evidence-Based Decisions

Consulting decisions are backed by data; therefore, your recommendation in the case interview should showcase your ability to make evidence-based decisions. First, define success using a list of metrics or brainstorming. Your interviewer understands that this is the first time you have seen the case—and they're likely working through the details themselves. As such, there's even less pressure to blaze through what should be a thoughtful exercise. Second, take creative risks. For a case that is fresh and unfamiliar to an interviewer, it's easy to win points by making a novel suggestion that your interviewer hadn't thought of yet.

There are, however, a few caveats.

- Don't assume that the interviewer is disinterested based on how they deliver the case. Interviewers get involved with recruiting because they care about finding talented individuals. That said, your interviewer is human and sometimes makes mistakes. Try not to judge a firm based on an interviewer's misstep.

- Don't assume that the interviewer will be more forgiving based on their lack of familiarity with the case. They are submersed in business problems like this case every day and will easily discover your strengths and weaknesses without studying the case for hours before the interview.

- If your interview is in the afternoon, your interviewer is likely to be more familiar with the case than if your interview is in the morning. In this scenario, creative recommendations become more important if you want your answers to stand out. They've likely heard the same handful of solutions from previous candidates that day.

and key performance indicators. Then, conduct a series of Day One dress rehearsals to measure each team's success rate in a low-risk environment. Finally, use those metrics to determine whether the merger is ready for execution ("go") or the client should invest additional time and money into integration planning ("no-go").

"I applied to McKinsey & Company after my undergraduate studies as an electrical engineer. In the first round of interviews, I was intimidated and thought the interviewers would set traps on every question. The truth was quite the opposite. The interviewers were helpful and even gave clues when I was struggling. My first takeaway from the interview experience is not to be afraid to ask questions, both regarding the case and the nature of the firm and your role. It is the most genuine way to show that you are interested. My second takeaway is to structure your responses. Take time to explain your thought process, even when making mathematical calculations. It's often more important than the result itself. Finally, act on the feedback that you get after the first round of interviews."

Eleftherios M., Associate, McKinsey & Company

Create a Sense of Resolution and Finality

Just as in the Maple Leaf case study, your case interview has a deadline. You have less than an hour to solve the case, and at the end you must make a recommendation.

Imagine that you came to Maple Leaf's "go/no-go" meeting without a recommendation for the leadership team. Or perhaps you make a "go" recommendation, but you also suggest a new performance management system for the bank based on challenges you uncovered working with the HR team. How do you expect leadership to react? In the first case, they may never work with you again because you didn't provide the answers that they hired you to provide. In the second case, they may scratch their heads and wonder why you went down a rabbit hole completely unrelated to the central challenge at hand.

That sense of frustration and confusion is how your interviewer will feel if you don't make a recommendation or if you answer a different question than the one originally posed during the interview. However, if you make a recommendation that clearly answers the original question, you will give a sense of resolution and finality to the case.

Act Like a Real-Life Consultant

At the end of a consulting case, you typically have a final meeting with the client to present your findings and discuss recommendations. By this point, the client usually knows what you're going to say because, hopefully, you've been working together to come up with a mutually agreeable solution. However, the final meeting serves an important purpose for both you and the client: to create a mutual sense of appreciation for the shared accomplishment.

The same concept is important during the case interview. You've been working with your interviewer throughout the case to determine and test hypotheses. By the end, you should both have a sense of the best solution to the case. However, stating that recommendation and reminding your interviewer how you collectively came to it will allow you both to appreciate the hard work and accomplishment of solving the case.

In the end, making a recommendation is icing on the cake. At that point in the interview, you've already put in the bulk of the hard work. Still, it's important to showcase your ability to make evidence-based decisions, create a sense of resolution to the case, and emulate what you will do as a consultant. Your recommendation should answer the original question—nothing else.

LEARNING TARGET:

◎ *Don't lose sight of the original question. Make sure your final recommendation answers the question posed initially.*

CASE INTERVIEW IN

2

DAYS

Mock Interview No. 9

Read through the following script with a friend or classmate. Next, review the instructions for live case practice on page 166. When ready, have your partner use the interview guide on page 179 to lead you through the case as if it were an actual interview.

Interviewer: *Gosworth & Sons is an international bank based in London that specializes in short-term security trading and long-term investment management for private entities such as family offices. After a recent recession, new regulations apply to the investment industry that have drastically reduced the scalability of security trading revenue, thereby affecting company profitability. With large cash reserves and a respected reputation, Gosworth & Sons is well positioned to navigate this hurdle in the near term. However, company management is concerned about long-term growth and has hired our team to identify opportunities to drive revenue in the future.*

Candidate: May I take a moment to review the information?

Interviewer: *Of course.*

Candidate: To be sure I haven't missed anything, I'm going to repeat the information I captured. Our client is Gosworth & Sons, a respected and stable international firm whose core business is short-term trading and long-term investing for private entities. New banking regulations have cut down on Gosworth's ability to produce sufficient revenue through security trading, causing leadership concern for the bank's future growth. In response, Gosworth & Sons has hired our team to identify new avenues for growth.

Interviewer: *That's it.*

Candidate: Great. I did have one question: could you define "family office"? I want to be sure I understand the type of customer Gosworth & Sons serves.

Interviewer: *Of course. Family offices are private wealth-management advisory firms that serve ultra-high-net-worth investors by providing a total outsourced solution to managing finances. For example, a family office may provide financial services related to investments, insurance, charitable giving, and taxes.*

Candidate: Interesting. So a family office would work with Gosworth & Sons to execute investing and trading strategies? What dollar amount qualifies an investor as ultra-high net worth?

Interviewer: *That's correct. Technically, Gosworth & Sons uses British pounds as its currency. By the client's definition, an investor must have assets of £200 million or more to be considered ultra-high net worth.*

Candidate: Do you mind if I take a moment to plan my approach?

Interviewer: *Go ahead; take your time.*

Candidate: Okay. Broadly speaking, Gosworth & Sons has two options for driving additional revenue growth: organic or inorganic. Organic growth could include increasing current revenue streams or developing new product offerings. Inorganic growth refers to acquiring new capabilities. To learn which of these avenues our client should take, I'd like to consider both internal and external factors that affect the company. First, we'll focus on Gosworth & Sons' current security trading and investment-management revenue streams to better understand the size, profitability, and growth of each. Next, I'd like to learn more about the external financial management market to better understand what other service offerings might exist that Gosworth & Sons doesn't yet provide. Finally, we'll compare the resources required to generate each growth opportunity, which will allow us to understand which one offers the best return on investment for Gosworth & Sons. Does this approach sound reasonable to you?

Interviewer: *It does.*

Candidate: Excellent. Starting with current revenue streams, do we have any information on the size, profitability, and growth trends for Gosworth & Sons' short-term security trading and long-term investment services?

Interviewer: *Investment services produced £8 billion in sales last year, after growing by 12 percent annually and netting 70 percent in profits each of the last 5 years. Security trading services produced £4.5 billion in sales last year, after averaging 6 percent growth on an annual basis and netting 55 percent in profits each of the last 5 years.*

Candidate: Hmm. As expected, security trading growth is obviously an issue. However, it seems that the effect of new regulations on trading profitability is getting lost in the averages. It's likely that profits were healthy for the first few years, but as the regulations came into effect, their effect was felt in the more recent years. Do we have more detailed data, broken down by year?

Interviewer: *We don't, but are regulations in fact affecting security trading profitability?*

Candidate: Well, we said that regulations are driving down trading revenue, which is affecting company profitability.

Interviewer: *Is company profitability the same as service-offering profitability?*

Candidate: Ah, I see what you mean. The issue is actually company profitability. That leads me to consider costs that affect the bank.

Interviewer: *What might these costs be? Are they fixed or variable? How does trading revenue affect overall company profitability?*

Candidate: I imagine that these are fixed costs such as salaries, office space, and entertainment for clients. In terms of the effect on profitability, it seems that lower trading revenue means fewer pounds to cover the overhead costs incurred by the company.

Interviewer: *Precisely.*

Candidate: That's helpful. With that in mind, let's transition to the external financial market. Are there other financial services being offered to family offices that Gosworth & Sons might consider adding to its portfolio?

Interviewer: *Given the legal structure, certifications, and expertise of Gosworth & Sons, there are no other services the client is viably able to provide to its customers.*

Candidate: That indicates to me that the only route toward company profitability is to reduce the company's fixed costs. As a firm serving ultra-high-net-worth private entities, Gosworth & Sons must maintain luxurious facilities and spend extravagantly on clients to win more business. Do we have any data related to these types of expenses?

Interviewer: *I'm going to stop you there before we go too deep down the rabbit hole. Let's remind ourselves by asking, What was the client's ask?*

Candidate: Identify new drivers of revenue for the future.

Interviewer: *Exactly. The client is more interested in growing sales than cutting overhead costs. While either lever can result in increased profitability, the expenses you mentioned are vital for*

Gosworth & Sons to maintain its prestige and serve its customer base. With that in mind, how can the client grow its revenues in the long run?

Candidate: Do you mind if I take a few seconds to collect my thoughts?

Interviewer: *Not a problem.*

Candidate: Okay. To recap, Gosworth & Sons is unable to offer new services to its family office customers, yet is interested in growing revenues to cover its fixed costs. If new services to current customers aren't a possibility, the next rational step is to find new customers. However, the population of family offices is likely small and already saturated by Gosworth & Sons and its competitors. Therefore, the other option for organic growth is targeting a different customer base. I hypothesize that Gosworth & Sons should focus on investment-management clients other than family offices. I'm thinking of high-net-worth individuals worth maybe £2 million to £200 million, as opposed to those of ultra-high net worth. To avoid confusion, let's refer to the ultra-high group as Alphas and the other group as Betas. Gosworth & Sons could leverage its facilities and expertise to serve the Beta clients, whose total count must be many times that of the Alphas, providing a substantial opportunity for future revenue growth. Assuming that Beta accounts produce decent profit margins, this new customer base will be able to cover the company's overhead expenses as well. Does that make sense?

Interviewer: *It does. I like where you're heading.*

Candidate: Great. Now let's see if the data supports my hypothesis. Do we have any information on the market size and profitability of investment-management services for Beta accounts?

Interviewer: *Let's assume that the world's population is 7 billion, and that Alpha and Beta customers together are 0.3 percent of the population. Alpha customers are the top 0.1 percent, and the remaining 0.2 percent are considered Betas, with an average of £5 million in assets, though only 10 percent of these are interested in having* *their wealth managed for them. These customers spend 1 percent of their total assets on investment-management services annually. The profit margin earned from these accounts by investment firms is 60 percent.*

Candidate: Okay, we'll take this one step at a time, starting with our population size. Betas represent 0.2 percent of the world's 7 billion population, or 14 million customers. Only 10 percent of these are potential customers, leaving us with 1.4 million customers, who have an average of £5 million in assets. Multiplying gives us £7 followed by 12 zeros. I believe that is £7 trillion?

Interviewer: *That's correct.*

Candidate: Great. Of that number, 1 percent is spent on investment services, which will give us our market size. If 10 percent of £7 trillion is £700 billion, then 1 percent is £70 billion. At that size, and with a 60 percent profit margin, it's safe to say that this is a viable and attractive market for Gosworth & Sons to target for future growth.

Interviewer: *What is Gosworth & Son's expected annual revenue growth rate if the firm can capture 4 percent of the Beta market by developing the required capabilities organically in 4 years? For ease of calculation, ignore the time value of money.*

Candidate: I know 7 multiplied by 4 is 28. That means that £70 billion multiplied by 40 percent must be £28 billion and by 4 percent is £2.8 billion. Compared to the company's total revenue last year of £12.5 billion, this represents about a 20 percent growth rate, or 5 percent annually over four years. Nothing special. How much would it cost Gosworth & Sons to build the service offering internally?

Interviewer: *About £1 billion.*

Candidate: Do we know how much market share Gosworth & Sons might capture if it were to acquire a Beta-focused investment firm? And at what cost?

Interviewer: *At a cost of £5 billion, Gosworth & Sons could capture twice as much market share in 2 years.*

Candidate: So that means 8 percent market share, or £5.6 billion, in 2 years. Comparing that figure to the company's total revenue last year of £12.5 billion, this represents about a 50 percent growth rate, or 25 percent annually over 2 years.

Interviewer: *Which option do you recommend?*

Candidate: Is it okay if I take a few minutes to gather my notes?

Interviewer: *No problem.*

Candidate: Great. As I've detailed in the slides I've sketched, we began our growth opportunity assessment by analyzing Gosworth & Sons' current revenue streams. Considering our client's focus on revenue growth to cover fixed costs, we hypothesized that the best path forward would be to target new clients in the Beta category. After running some calculations, we can compare two options for seizing the market opportunity. Option A is to grow this service offering organically, earning an annual revenue growth rate of 5 percent and profits of £1.8 billion over 4 years. Option B is to acquire a firm already in the space, resulting in an annual growth rate of nearly 25 percent and profits of £5.6 billion in two years. Based purely on the financials, I recommend that Gosworth & Sons choose Option B. Further, there are nonfinancial benefits that make this route appealing. First, Gosworth & Sons could gain knowledge of the Beta-customer segment, which may be different from the company's Alpha customers. Second, Gosworth & Sons could acquire a firm that expands its geographical reach, allowing for new opportunities among the Alpha population. Third, while Gosworth & Sons may not be well-known beyond the Alpha realm today, acquiring a Beta-focused firm will allow Gosworth & Sons to immediately enter that market by leveraging the acquisition's already established reputation.

Interviewer: *Well said. What are a few risks involved in making such an acquisition?*

Candidate: One potential hazard is that the underlying assumptions used in our calculations are flawed, which could result in our client over-paying for their new capabilities. From what I've read in business news, overpaying is a common characteristic of large acquisitions. Another is the risk that top talent from the acquisition may choose to join a dif-ferent firm rather than work for Gosworth & Sons, which would greatly diminish the value of the purchase. To address this risk, we would need to assist our client in careful planning and execution of the deal to retain top talent. One way would be providing new employees with ample sup-port and giving them a voice throughout the transition.

Interviewer: *Both are great examples. Well done. That concludes our case. In the minute we have left, is there anything more that you'd like to share about your interest in our consulting firm?*

Candidate: I'm glad you asked. Your firm is definitely my top choice. I've really enjoyed getting to meet your team during the various recruiting events. Based on the conversations I've had, your firm seems to be a per-fect personal fit for my values, interests, and goals. Thank you for your time, and I look forward to hearing back soon!

Interviewer: *Well, we've enjoyed getting to know you as well. The recruiting process certainly isn't easy, but I think you've navigated it just fine.*

20 19 18 17 16 15
14 13 12 11 10 9 8
7 6 5 4 3 2 1

1

Rest, Read, and Relax

After 20 days of case preparation, your interview is tomorrow. Are you ready? How do you feel mentally? Physically? Emotionally? Reflecting on your hard work to date, you should feel confident in your skills and ready to walk into the interview room tomorrow with poise and self-assurance.

Today, you have only three tasks: rest, read, and relax.

At this point, you've learned all of the skills and tricks you need to succeed. You've applied those skills over the course of nine mock case interviews and allowing your mind to absorb the important concepts and techniques. There's no need to cram during the final 24 hours before your interview—none of the new material is likely to stick in such a short period of time. Therefore, your focus today should be solely on refreshing your mind, body, and spirit so that you walk into tomorrow's interview calm yet energized.

Rest

During interview preparation, you may have discovered that your mind wasn't the only part of you that felt exhausted at the end of the day.

Booz Allen Hamilton is considered a critical advisor to the United States government, having aligned itself to this service beginning in the 1940s. Today, the firm receives more than 95 percent of its revenue from the US federal government. With expertise on executing IT strategy and organizational change, the firm is involved across the entire federal ecosystem, ranging from secretive military projects to public infrastructure analyses. Having separated itself from the commercial branch Booz & Company in early 2008, the firm went public in November 2010, though the private equity firm Carlyle Group remains a majority shareholder.

Interview preparation is also physically and emotionally demanding. You spend hours hunched over books or become tense during mock interviews. The uncertainty and pressure of job searching is emotionally stressful. Today is a day to purge yourself of any mental, physical, and emotional challenges you're experiencing.

Clear your mind: Forget about frameworks, calculations, and business cases for today. Try 15 minutes of meditation: Sit or lie in a comfortable position, inhale deeply for 5 seconds, and exhale completely for 5 seconds. Think of a word or phrase to repeat in your head as a mantra, such as "drive," "energy," or "confidence." Pick something that you want to focus on and bring to the interview.

Be active, but don't overdo it: Don't do any strenuous exercise that might make you sore the next day. Instead, devote some time to walking or jogging, outdoors if possible, and spend at least 20 minutes stretching or practicing yoga afterward. Make sure your neck, shoulders, and back feel loose and relaxed. Focus on releasing tension in areas where you tend to hold it.

Eat a nutritious meal: Avoid fried foods, salty snacks, and sugary sweets. Drink five 8-ounce glasses of water: one with each meal, one during exercise, and one before bed.

All the preparation you've done up to this point will be magnified if you go into the interview with a positive and energetic mind, body, and spirit. Focus on recuperation today by prioritizing meditation, physical activity, and "me" time.

Read

Along with the case portion of tomorrow's interview, you will converse with peers and employees throughout the day. Your interviewer is likely to ask you a few personal questions before diving into the case, and you may find yourself engaging in side conversations about current events or recent local happenings. As such, today you should read a few of your favorite news outlets to brush up on events.

If you don't read the *Wall Street Journal* every day, that's okay. Don't start today. Instead, peruse your favorite news outlets, and pick a variety of topics. Check out *People* magazine. Read about your favorite sports

MY INTERVIEW STORY

"After majoring in computer science, I realized that I didn't want a job where I would be stuck in a cubicle all day writing code. I was drawn to consulting as it allowed me variability like no other traditional coding job would. During my work with KPMG, no two projects that I was on were similar, and that often posed its own set of challenges. What often amazed me was how the firm was committed to investing in its employees and setting them up for success in the long term. Apart from the internal training resources available for reference, every middle-management employee in the practice was tasked with training associates for a set number of hours on a variety of topics ranging from advanced Excel to technical concepts to risk formalities. Armed with this knowledge, I was able to not only add value to clients but also steer my career in the direction I wanted by actively requesting to be on projects of my choice and interest."

Swati S., Business Process Analyst, KPMG Consulting

team. Skim the local newspaper. Look up CNN on Instagram for a snapshot view into international news. Your objective should not be to cram every current event into your mind. Instead, focus on updating yourself about relevant topics that align with your interests and that you would feel comfortable discussing with your interviewer.

Additionally, reread your résumé. Your interviewer is likely to have it with her during the interview, and she may ask you questions about your experiences. Be prepared for this. For example, if you've listed "Boys & Girls Club mentor" under leadership, prepare an anecdote or lesson you learned from that experience.

Finally, spend an hour reading your current or favorite book today. Reading for fun will help relax you. Books are also an excellent conversation topic for interview day. As with current events, pick a book that you actually like and that aligns with your personality. Don't languish over a classic novel or financial journal simply because you think it will make you sound smart.

Relax

Your final task is to relax. Have a glass of wine. Go to bed early. Get no less than eight hours of sleep. Set your alarm to give you plenty of time to get ready in the morning. The easiest way to undermine your hard work is to rush into an interview panicked, sweaty, and flustered. Instead, arrive a minimum of 30 minutes early to give yourself ample time to chat with greeters and other candidates. Doing so will reduce your stress level.

"Alt-travel" is travel taken by a consultant from the client to a location other than their home city. This benefit allows consultants to fly to family events or exotic locales on the client's dime but only if the cost is equal to or less than the cost of flying home.

Tomorrow is an important day. You've put in 20 days of hard work, discipline, and repetition to get to where you are today. Now is the time to rest, read, and relax to ensure that you arrive fresh to the interview and leave confident that you put on your best performance and showed your interviewer that you've got what it takes. Good luck!

Appendix A:

Live Case Practice: Interviewer Guides

Without a doubt, the best method of preparing for a case interview is to practice live cases where you can experience the time constraints and pressures associated with an actual interview. Below are instructions for you and your partner to use the interview guides on the following pages.

Interviewer Instructions:

- Using the interview guides provided in the following pages, begin by providing the initial case information (client and industry) to the candidate, then state the issue and client goal.

- Share only the requested information, but steer the candidate back in the right direction if he or she gets off track. Remember, interviewers rarely confuse candidates intentionally; the best practice is to serve as a guide as the candidate works through the case.

- Once complete, discuss any positive highlights from their performance, as well as any areas that need development.

Candidate Instructions:

- Set a timer for 45 minutes, which is the typical time for case interviews (not including any introductions or small talk). Make sure you allow yourself five minutes to give your final recommendation.

- Do the interview as you would on the actual day—including taking notes, making mental calculations, asking for time to process your thoughts, and providing a summary of findings and a recommendation. Challenge yourself to come up with alternate solutions and recommendations from the scripted interview.

- At the end of the interview, compare your performance with the case script from the relevant chapter to see how another candidate may have handled the case.

Case Interview in 18 Days: Mock Interview No. 1

CLIENT NAME	BullDoze Inc.
INDUSTRY	Heavy machinery manufacturing
HEADQUARTERS	Indiana, USA
ISSUE BACKGROUND	Over the past 5 years, BullDoze has seen average annual revenue growth of 12% while operating in 24 markets in South America, Africa, and the Middle East. However, revenue growth across those geographies is projected to drop by 50% within the next 3 years.
CLIENT GOAL	Identify new growth opportunities in emerging markets.
PRODUCT	Backhoes, bulldozers
CUSTOMERS	~80% construction companies, ~15% governments, ~5% individuals (e.g., farmers)
REVENUE	$5 billion last year
COMPETITORS	Global players that focus predominately on the developed markets in North America, Europe, Australia, and Japan. They have the most advanced, powerful equipment available, and charge 20% more than our client does.
CLIENT MANUFACTURING	Closest facility is in Pakistan, on the Indian Ocean coast. The cost to ship 1 piece of construction equipment (e.g., bulldozer) is $100 per mile. There are 3,000 miles between the factory and the nearest port in southeast Asia. To build a new facility, it would cost $250 million and take 3 years.
NEW GROWTH OPPORTUNITY	The governments of Cambodia, Myanmar, Thailand, and Vietnam are on the verge of announcing plans to build an international highway system to better facilitate trade. The system will stretch to all four corners of the region, leading to India in the northwest and China in the northeast. Initial construction is expected to begin within the next 2 years. About $10 billion is expected to be spent on the project, though no company has yet been awarded the contract.

CLIENT NAME	Body Surf Hotel
INDUSTRY	Cabana lodging and private surf lessons: "Cabana lodging" is lodging where the guest stays in a small bungalow or house as opposed to a room. This provides the guest with increased privacy and space.
HEADQUARTERS	Three Central American countries
ISSUE BACKGROUND	Leading their region in social media marketing, the company has enjoyed increasingly high levels of popularity. The company's marketing team produces a creative, entertaining travel blog that has caught on in the amateur surf community. However, over the past few years, the company has struggled to earn a profit.
CLIENT GOAL	Identify the profitability issue and provide a set of potential solutions.
CUSTOMERS	The majority of Body Surf Hotel's guests are health-conscious young adults from the United States and Canada. In the high season, Body Surf Hotel receives about 200 guests per month, and in the low season, the number is closer to 100. High and low season are split equally across the year, 6 months each.
PRODUCT	Body Surf Hotel sells only one product: overnight surf packages.
PRICING	$6,000 per person
REVENUE	The business has seen a decline in customer purchases each of the past 3 years.
FIXED EXPENSES	Salary: $570,000 Utilities: $10,000 Other: $20,000 Total: $600,000
VARIABLE EXPENSES	Each guest costs Body Surf Hotel $2,000 per stay. This includes transportation to and from the airport, food, cleaning, depreciation of surfing equipment, and T-shirts provided by the company. Last year, the company added 4 extra meals per guest at a cost of $10 per meal, which is included in the $2000 total.
COMPETITORS	Other local operators have increased sales over the same time period. The average price for overnight surf hotels with structured activities is $4,000.

Case Interview in 14 Days: Mock Interview No. 3

CLIENT NAME	Swirl Tech Inc.
INDUSTRY	Medical device manufacturing: Medical devices company that manages the product development process, from testing to mass commercial production.
HEADQUARTERS	Seattle, Washington, USA
ISSUE BACKGROUND	Swirl Tech is in the final stages of developing a new generation of its product. Due to its cutting-edge nature, the product is projected to generate strong sales when released. The company is receiving pressure from its venture partners to release the product quickly.
CLIENT GOAL	Determine when the product should be launched.
CUSTOMERS	50% directly to physicians, 50% to hospitals and clinics
PRODUCT	The company's core product line specializes in devices that produce a virtual overlay of various measurements and data for surgeons to use while looking through a microscope. Similar to the displays currently used in fighter jets and luxury automobiles, the additional data reduces the need to look away from the patient, dramatically reducing the incidence of human error during a procedure.
PRICING	$60,000 per unit
REVENUE	The estimated unit sales for the product launch in 1, 2, and 3 years are 500, 400, and 200, respectively ($30 million, $24 million, and $12 million).
PREVIOUS LAUNCHES	The first project began development 4 years ago. Each new generation has taken about 2 years to develop and sell commercially. The first generation wasn't adopted quickly and had a high failure rate, leading to frustrated surgeons and high replacement costs for Swirl Tech. Major improvements were made in the second generation, and sales doubled over the course of 2 years.
	The current version of the product represents the third generation. It is about 90% complete and has been in development and testing for a little under a year. This version provides more customization and sophistication. However, so far there has been limited time to solicit feedback from Key Opinion Leaders (KOLs). In the life sciences industry, KOLs are top doctors that team with companies to help develop better products.

continues on next page

FAILURE RATES AND ASSOCIATED COSTS	3-year development timeline = 0.5% failure rate = $2 million in costs
	2-year development timeline = 2% failure rate = $12 million in costs
	1-year development timeline = 5% failure rate = $25 million in costs
COMPETITORS	There is one other major player that makes less sophisticated virtual overlays. That company has recently made large investments in their research and development department and are presumed to have the capability to create a comparably advanced product within the next 24 months.

Case Interview in 12 Days: Mock Interview No. 4

CLIENT NAME	Aussie Alpine
INDUSTRY	Ski resort
HEADQUARTERS	Southern Australia
ISSUE BACKGROUND	Aussie Alpine leads the national ski resort market in revenue. Despite its market dominance, the company has experienced stagnant top-line growth, and its leadership team is growing concerned that competitors may soon catch up.
CLIENT GOAL	Identify a remedy for Aussie Alpine's growth issues.
PRODUCT	Ski slopes, terrain parks, ski shops, restaurants, condos, and retail outlets. During the winter, ski customers use the summit restaurant from dawn until dusk each day, leaving no time available for event hosting. The lodging and restaurant facilities can operate at a maximum capacity of 500 people.
PRICING	Prices have remained level over the past 3 to 5 years. Aussie Alpine is a high-volume resort, which is achieved by maintaining lower prices compared to other operators in the area. The prices at the various retail outlets can't be lowered any further from their current positions. Otherwise, the company would become cash-flow negative.
VOLUME	The park overall has seen a steady flow of visitors over the past several years, with an average annual growth rate in the low single digits. This trend is echoed throughout the various park outlets as well.
REVENUE	About $350 million in total sales each winter
MARKET SIZE	The Australian ski market consists of about 2.1 million skier visits annually. The average skier visit produces $308 in revenue (2.1 million x ~300 = $630 million). The Australian ski market is fully saturated and has grown at a steady pace over the past 3 to 5 years.
SUMMER MONTH ACTIVITIES	Repairing, rebuilding, or expanding their current assets. The restaurants, bars, and condos at the mountain's base remain open for business. Retail stores are closed for the summer season, as are the slopes, hotels, and the single summit restaurant.

Case Interview in 10 Days: Mock Interview No. 5

CLIENT NAME	Longhorn Oil Corp.
INDUSTRY	Integrated multinational oil and gas: "Integrated" is short for vertically integrated, which means the company operates multiple steps within the energy supply chain, as opposed to just one. For example, Longhorn Oil not only discovers and extracts natural resources, but it also transports and refines those resources later in the supply chain.
HEADQUARTERS	The company operates in 47 countries and has corporate headquarters in Houston, Dubai, São Paulo, and Singapore.
ISSUE BACKGROUND	With more than 60,000 employees, Longhorn has substantial assets that make it a dominant player in its field. An important challenge of Longhorn's size, however, is the slow speed at which the company can adjust to innovative moves made by its competitors. Recently, another major energy firm announced a new initiative to invest in renewable energy. Specifically, the competitor is planning to spend $5 billion over the next 3 years on wind and solar farms in an effort to diversify its energy holdings and generate goodwill with the public. Our client's leadership team is concerned that Longhorn Oil may miss out on the opportunities of tomorrow.
CLIENT GOAL	Assess whether the company should enter the renewable energy market.
REVENUE	~$200 billion annual revenue
COMPETITORS	Through a federal government program, our competitor will be allowed to write off taxes on all $5 billion spent on their project.
RENEWABLE ENERGY DETAIL	Without subsidies, wind and solar power can't be produced profitably at this time. However, researchers estimate that, within a decade, scientists will develop the technology necessary to efficiently capture and store renewable energy, making it competitive with oil or gas.

CLIENT EXPERIENCE IN RENEWABLE ENERGY	Our client had an unsuccessful foray into thermal energy 6 years ago. Since then, management has focused purely on oil and natural gas. In regards to a research team, Longhorn Oil has no strong candidates within its ranks to execute the effort.
INDUSTRY DETAILS	Concerning financials, mergers, and failures, the industry has experienced nothing outside the norm from the standard oil and gas cyclicality experienced throughout the last several decades. There have been some tech breakthroughs related to renewable energy, but none have resulted in a scalable, profitable energy platform. There have been discoveries of new oil and gas fields, both offshore and through the hydraulic fracturing of shale, also known as "fracking."
POTENTIAL ACQUISITION TARGET	A company based in San Diego that is considered the most innovative developer of wind and solar energy technology. We know from analyst reports that in 5 years the California-based company is expected to generate $84 million in annual sales. The standard valuation multiple used is 45 times revenue. In finance, we use what are called "valuation multiples" to quickly estimate the value of an enterprise. Simply put, the multiple is a multiplier applied to a given company's revenue. Each industry has a different range of possible multiples based on future growth prospects and considering past performance.
POTENTIAL ACQUISITION VALUE	$84 million × 45 multiple = ($80 million × 40) + ($80 million × 5) + ($4 million × 40) + ($4 million × 5) = $3.2 billion + $400 million + $160 million + $20 million = $3.78 billion

Case Interview in 8 Days: Mock Interview No. 6

CLIENT NAME	Telechatter Inc.
INDUSTRY	Telecommunications
HEADQUARTERS	Seattle, Washington, USA
ISSUE BACKGROUND	Operating a nationwide network of cellular towers, Telechatter competes with a handful of domestic competitors to relay data to and from customers' devices. Despite their strong position, over the past 2 years Telechatter has experienced a decline in sales that threatens to derail the company's 5-year strategic plan.
CLIENT GOAL	Determine the cause of the revenue decline and identify a potential solution.
CUSTOMERS	Individuals and families make up 73% of customers, and organizations such as businesses and governments make up 27%. The company's satisfaction rates have remained competitive across the nation except for the Mountain West region, which has seen a 41% decline. This region is composed of mountain towns from Montana to Colorado and one major city, Denver. All regions share the same offshore customer service team.
PRODUCT	Cellular communication plans
PRICING	Individual plans cost $80 per year, family plans cost $100 per year, and business plans cost $150 per year. None of these prices have changed recently.
VOLUME	Telechatter's customer base dropped by 2 million customers 2 years ago and 1 million customers last year. All three plan types have experienced a decline in sales. None of the plans' content has changed within the last 2 years.
MARKET SIZE	Telechatter services 10% of the American population.
COMPETITORS	The overall market has continued to grow, while the competitive landscape has remained relatively static. Telechatter has been the dominant player in the Mountain West region for nearly a decade, but two other service providers have been in the area for the same period of time. We don't have reliable competitor data by geography, but anecdotally, these less popular service providers seem to have experienced an uptick in sales over the past 2 years.

MOUNTAIN WEST REGION DETAILS	There have been no significant damage, hardware upgrades, or software changes related to the Mountain West towers. The only notable physical development near the client's towers is a new military base 50 miles from Denver.
	We are aware that cellular signals can be interrupted by certain radio frequencies. We also know that military bases are heavy users of such radio frequencies, and that the timing of the disruption aligns fairly closely with the establishment of the base.
TOWER RELOCATION DETAILS	The cost of relocating the cellular tower near Denver is $15 million.
	Assume that the entire customer volume drop is attributable to the greater Denver metro area and only 20% of customers would return if service returns to the previous standard.
	Assume that plan types are split evenly across the customer population, and each product type earns a profit margin of 10%.
TOTAL COST OF FORGOING TOWER RELOCATION	Prices: $80 + $100 + $150 = $330 / 3 = $110 average price
	Cost of not relocating = 3 million customers × $110 average price = $330 million revenue
	$330 million × 10% profit margin = $33 million in forgone annual profits
TOTAL COST OF RELOCATING TOWER	$33 million in forgone annual profits × 20% customer re-signed to plans = $6.6 million recovered annually
	$15 million cost of relocation ÷ $6.6 million recovered annually = 2–3 year payback period

Case Interview in 6 Days: Mock Interview No. 7

CLIENT NAME	State Department of Corrections (DOC)
INDUSTRY	Correctional institutions (e.g., jails, prisons)
ISSUE BACKGROUND	Due to recent budget cuts, DOC leadership has been asked to reduce prison expenditures by 10% in 1 year. With a current annual cost per inmate that is already 15% lower than the national average, the state prison system is struggling to identify additional opportunities for cutting costs.
CLIENT GOAL	Reduce the $2 billion budget by 10% while still maintaining adequate care and security for prisoners.

BUDGET BREAKDOWN	**Fixed**	**Variable**	
	50% security and security personnel wages	20% medical	5% laundry
		15% food	5% parole activities
	5% admin/other		

COST PER INMATE AFTER BUDGET CUT	$2 billion × 90% = $1.8 billion $1.8 billion ÷ 60,000 inmates = $30,000 per inmate annually
CURRENT COST PER MEAL	$2 billion × 15% = $300 million $300 million ÷ 60,000 inmates = $5,000 per inmate for food each year $5,000 ÷ 365 = ~$15 per day ÷ 3 meals per day = ~$5 per meal
DOC SYSTEM SIZE	93 jail facilities, 22 prisons, 63,000 inmates
SECURITY DETAILS	Security is government employees. The DOC system has several teams it employs across the state to manage things like construction, maintenance, security tests, and camera installations for all of its facilities. Leadership is not interested in cutting any security expenses at this time.

MEDICAL DETAILS	Salaries are tightly regulated to ensure prisoners receive adequate healthcare. The state's politicians are careful to mitigate the risk of bad press stemming from sick prisoners.
FOOD/LAUNDRY SERVICE DETAILS	Food and laundry are run by private contractors. Based on market rates, it would cost $1.50 to $2.00 per meal to feed the DOC inmates using an outsourcer. On average, laundry costs would be cut by $100,000 per facility annually. Both of these figures include reduced headcount of workers.
COMPETITOR PRISON COSTS	A neighboring state has one of the cheapest cost-per-inmate rates in the country at $15,000. This is due in large part to successful labor negotiations and outsourcing of healthcare to private providers, mostly low-volume doctors from the rural areas surrounding the prison facilities. Such physicians have lower bill rates and are often asked to cover multiple facilities within a given radius by scheduling once-a-week visits. Mortality rates compared to those at DOC are 22% higher.

Case Interview in 4 Days: Mock Interview No. 8

CLIENT NAME	McSweet's Eats
INDUSTRY	Baked goods
ISSUE BACKGROUND	The company recently won a major sports contract that allows it to operate within a broad network of college and professional football stadiums over the next 2 years, retaining 60% of the profits it generates. Based on McSweet's Eats' profitability during this trial period, the football stadium network may extend their contract by 10 years. If McSweet's Eats isn't able to contribute an average of $20,000 in profits to each stadium in the network, the contract will expire and a different vendor will take its place. The company's management team is confident that they can produce and distribute enough product to fulfill their contract, but they are nervous that football fans might be difficult to win over when there are more traditional food options available.
CLIENT GOAL	Develop a marketing strategy to maximize sales throughout the trial period.
PRODUCT	McSweet's Eats makes gourmet cookie arrangements. Included is a dozen cookies on stems, plastic-wrapped together and set in a small box that serves as a base. The most basic offering consists of one type of cookie, either sugar or chocolate chip, while the premium selection includes 12 unique gourmet cookies.
BASIC OPTION PRICING	50¢ per cookie $2 for the base $1 for the plastic wrap 10¢ per stem	(50¢ + 10¢) x 12 + $2 +$1 = (60¢ × 12) + $2 + $1 = $10.20 per basic arrangement
VOLUME	There are about 80,000 fans at any given college or professional football game. There is an average of 10 games per regular season per stadium.
COMPETITORS	Cotton candy sells for $8. Ice cream bars sell for $7.
SALES OUTLET	The contract only allows for walking vendors. Each stadium determines the number of walking vendors.

Case Interview in 2 Days: Mock Interview No. 9

CLIENT NAME	Gosworth & Sons
INDUSTRY	Financial services
HEADQUARTERS	London, UK
ISSUE BACKGROUND	After a recent recession, new regulations apply to the investment industry that have drastically reduced the scalability of security trading revenues, thereby affecting company profitability. With large cash reserves and a respected reputation, Gosworth & Sons is well positioned to navigate this hurdle in the near term. However, company management is concerned about long-term growth.
CLIENT GOAL	Identify opportunities to drive future revenue.
CUSTOMERS	Private entities such as family offices. Family offices are private wealth-management advisory firms that serve ultra-high-net-worth investors by providing a total outsourced solution to managing finances. For example, a family office may provide financial services related to investments, insurance, charitable giving, and taxes.
	An investor must have assets of £200 million or more to be considered ultra-high net worth. These investors represent the top 0.1% of the 7 billion people in the world in terms of wealth.
	The remaining investors in the top 0.3% of the population have an average of £5 million in assets. Ten percent of these use wealth-management firms, which costs 1% of their total assets on investment-management services annually. The profit margin earned from these accounts by investment firms is 60%.

PRODUCT PERFORMANCE		Short-term security trading	Long-term investment management
	Revenue (prior year)	£8 billion	£4.5 billion
	5 Year Avg. Revenue Growth	12%	6%
	5 Year Avg. Profit Margin	70%	55%

SERVICE-OFFERING CONSIDERATIONS	Given the legal structure, certifications, and expertise of Gosworth & Sons, there are no other services the client is viably able to provide to its customers.
	It would cost £1 billion to expand into the Beta category organically and 4 years to capture 4% market share.
	It would cost £5 billion to acquire a Beta-focused firm and 2 years to capture 8% market share.

Appendix B:
Industries and Services

Industry Insights

Consumer and Industrial Products

Consumer and industrial products cover a broad range of the items we see and use every day. Whether a company sells shampoo, skateboards, tables, or tractors, competition in this space is fierce and characterized by wildly fluctuating trends, complex international supply chains, and demanding consumers. Interviewers expect to see more rigor and creativity from candidates during such cases. Additionally, these types of cases typically will require you to pay attention to consumer wants and needs when developing pricing strategies, branding campaigns, and market size estimates.

Energy and Natural Resources

The energy and natural resources industry encompasses companies such as international oil and gas companies, solar panel manufacturers, electric utilities, and even gold miners. In general, it's known for massive capital expenditures, fluctuating commodity prices, and long-term project timelines. Energy and natural resources clients typically use consultants for operations management, risk advisory, and restructuring. Companies in this space often face heavy political and public scrutiny. Keep this in mind when navigating cases, and be sure to consider any government regulations that might limit the strategic options available to company leaders.

Financial Services

The financial services industry spans a wide range of businesses, including commercial banks, investment banks, insurance brokerages, private equity firms, and hedge funds. What they have in common is the facilitation of business through the management of money. Cases on this industry are often difficult due to the financial jargon and regulatory implications. Don't be afraid to ask your interviewer clarifying questions if you're unfamiliar with any terms or regulations in the case.

Healthcare/Life Sciences

Healthcare/life sciences refers to businesses focused on health and longevity of life. Healthcare, including health insurance and hospital chains, is consumer centric, heavily regulated, and highly politicized. Life science companies, including pharmaceuticals and medical devices, develop and sell health-related products. They tend to be at the cutting edge of technology and spend massive amounts of capital on research and development. For cases dealing with healthcare or life sciences, be prepared to explain how the various organizations interact with one another within the health ecosystem.

Public Sector

The public sector refers to government agencies and departments, whether they are federal, state, or local. Including a diverse range of topics from national defense to national parks, the public sector industry uses consultants in unique ways. Regulations and bureaucracy often result in multi-year projects worth millions of dollars. When considering a government-oriented case, be sure that your recommendation is realistic in terms of timeframe for execution and the risk appetite of your client.

Social Impact

One of the hottest sectors in consulting, the social impact industry consists of nonprofit organizations, philanthropic organizations, and for-profit companies that espouse corporate responsibility. Rather than being purely profit-driven, this industry is community oriented, whether at the local level or through massive international initiatives. Balancing lofty aspirations and financial constraints, social impact consultants often focus on how their clients can make an efficient, effective impact with limited resources. Be conscious of the cost-benefit ratio of various scenarios when analyzing a case in this industry.

Services Sold

Human Capital

The focus of human capital consulting is people: how to organize, empower, lead, and inspire people. For companies big and small, the human component is often the most challenging. How many employees are needed? What skills do they need? How should they be structured into teams? How can we retain more employees? How can we better develop our employees? Human capital consultants leverage research, data, and insights to answer such questions and optimize the relationship between employees and employer. When answering any case question, it's good practice to consider if there is a human capital issue affecting the business.

Information Technology

Information technology (IT) consulting is the practice of developing or improving the flow of information, either within an organization or between a company and the outside world. Broad in scope, the IT function handles everything from customer receipts to employee health plans to vendor payments. It's no wonder that the IT consulting space is massive, as the disruption of any of these client activities can quickly cause real harm to the business. In your case work, rather than treating IT as a back-office activity, be sure to highlight the function's vital enabling qualities.

Mergers, Acquisitions, and Divestitures

Mergers, acquisitions, and divestitures refer to the reorganization of two or more entities through consolidation (mergers and acquisitions, or M&A) or deconsolidation (divestiture). With consolidation, a company is adding scale, geographical reach, and new capabilities. With deconsolidation, a company is selling a business unit that is costly or misaligned with their core competency. Mergers, acquisitions, and divestitures are risky and often fail. As such, clients use consultants for due diligence, pre-deal planning, and post-deal integration to mitigate risk of failure. For cases on this topic, be sure that you're able to justify the cost of acquisition compared to the cost of organic growth.

Operational Improvement

Operational improvement refers to the analysis of business processes in the search for greater efficiency and increased production. Whether it's an international supply chain or a customer service procedure, operational performance management is a vital exercise that can make the difference between a profitable and a failed company. When a Fortune 500 organization saves a few dollars on the cost of a product or cuts several minutes from a manufacturing process, the ripple effects can add millions of dollars to the company's bottom line. Don't belittle the multiplier effect of pennies and seconds when navigating an operational improvement case.

Strategy

Sound strategic consulting stems from rigorous data analytics, diversity of thought, exhaustive consumer studies, and imaginative thought exercises. This last point is important to remember during a strategy-oriented case; no multi-billion dollar company hires consultants to hear what they already know. Be bold with your suggestions, leveraging your creativity to stand out from other candidates.

Sustainability

Another hot topic in business today is sustainability, or the affect a business has on the environment and community. With references of the "triple bottom line" (social, environmental, financial) growing more and more prominent among investors, it's no wonder that many corporate boardrooms have taken up the mantle of leading the sustainability movement. Consulting solutions for this area focus on problems such as energy inefficiency, water contamination, and community disruption. While each should be measured in dollars, it's important during the case to highlight the human effects as well.

Index

P

Passive promotion, 141–142, 145
Pasteur, Louis, 21
Peers, networking with, 87
People, in internal/external
    framework, 53
Perservance, in being successful in
    case interviews, 136
Photos, positing of, on social
    media, 71
Physical activity, 162–163
Point, making, in case interview,
    146–151
Popularity, volume and, 42
Porter's Five Forces, 66
Positioning, 139–141
Practitioners, networking of, 87
Predictions, making moderate, 85
Preparation, in being successful in
    case interviews, 136
Presentation format, 39
Pressure-testing, 115
Price(s)
    as factor in revenue, 33–34, 43, 75
    optimizing, 139
    in profitability framework, 88–89
    sensitivity of, 28
Price elasticity, 48
Price-sensitivity analysis, 133
PricewaterhouseCoopers, 35, 68
Pricing, competitive, 25, 68–69
Probing questions, 101–102, 104, 131
Problem solving, 6
Process, in internal/external
    framework, 54
Product(s), 139
    development of, 58
    expansion of offerings, 77–78
    in internal/external
        framework, 53
    positioning, 68–69, 72
Product portfolio, 107

Product-quality standards, 60
Profit
    in profitability framework, 35, 38
    revenue and, 35
Profit margin, 46–47
Profitability
    analysis of, 47–48, 133
    analysis of decline in, 46
    company, 155
    launch timing and, 59–60
    revenue and costs in driving,
        42–43
    service-offering, 155
Profitability framework, 32, 36–37,
    66, 130
    application to case, 38–39
    costs in, 34–35
    price in, 88–89
    profit in, 35, 38
    revenue in, 33–34, 88–89
    volume in, 88–89
Promotions. *See also* Advertising;
    Social media
    active, 141–142, 145
    passive, 141–142, 145
Public sector, 39, 181
    reducing headcount in, 122,
        124–125
Punctuality in case interviews, 70

Q

Qualitative information, 116, 118
Quantitative analysis, 131
Quantitative information, 116, 118
Quantitative questions, 102
Quantitative skills, 36
Question marks, 100
Questions
    asking, in case interviews, 71, 164
    balancing the asking of, with
        making inferences, 15
    clarifying, 92, 100–101, 104, 139

Acknowledgments

To our family and friends, who always put up with us: We love you. Please forgive our over-caffeinated behavior while writing this book. We never could have done this (or anything else, really!) without you.

To our brilliant mentors, who have shaped us into the businesspeople and teammates we are today: You know who you are, and we are forever in your debt.

To the generous firm leaders, who endured our case interviews and decided to take a chance on us anyway: We hope this book is proof of how we've grown under your guidance.